Lionheart Catholic

How to Become a Saint in These Dark Times

Lionheart Catholic
How to Become a Saint in These Dark Times

Copyright © 2019 Devin Rose

This is to all the Lionheart Catholics who read the fine print...well played.

Published by Devoted Coders, LLC

ISBN: 978-0-578-53914-0 (Paperback Edition)
Printed in the United States of America

Cover Design: Kvetka Designs, LLC

Lionheart Catholic

How to Become a Saint in These Dark Times

Devin Rose

Devoted Coders, LLC
Round Rock, Texas

Dedication

To my lionhearted wife, Catherine
And to Edmund and Josephine, my little Lionhearts

TABLE OF CONTENTS

CHAPTER 1

A Time of Confusion

I remember in 2013 when Pope Francis was elected to the papacy.

I was surprised and excited. Here was a bishop who I had never heard of, one who seemed humble and unassuming. I looked forward to what new ideas he might bring to the papacy and to the Church.

My wife and I, along with our two young children, were watching on the computer live-feed as he walked out onto the balcony from the "room of tears" and humbly bowed before everyone gathered at St. Peter's Square.

We then watched the Catholic pundits as they scrambled to figure out who this new pope was, where he came from, and what theme he might have for his pontificate. It was clear that they had been caught flat-footed by who the Cardinals had elected as the new pope.

As the months went by, I eagerly read everything that Pope Francis wrote, interviews while on the airplane, Wednesday audiences, looking for indications of what perspective he was coming from.

Papal Perplexity

I jumped to his defense when he seemed to say confusing things in his talks. Because I had known and loved Pope John Paul II and Pope Benedict, I figured that Pope Francis was going to be cut from the same cloth as they were. I gave him the benefit of the doubt and sought to read the full transcripts of his words, as well as any justifications from trustworthy Catholic sources on what was actually said.

At first I thought that his head-scratching statements were exceptional situations, where enemies of the church were taking his words out of context and twisting them for their own benefit. But I became perplexed as a pattern emerged: it seemed that every opportunity he had, he was saying something that was confusing (or borderline heretical).

Having come into the Church during Pope John Paul II's papacy, and then enjoying the eight years of Pope Benedict's reign, the idea that the pope would be anything but a stalwart champion of orthodoxy was unthinkable to me.

But was the unthinkable now happening?

I dug below the surface, and started to learn of Pope Francis's other actions: he was demoting and sacking good priests and bishops, and promoting heterodox ones instead. Bit by bit, he was dismantling what Pope John Paul II and Pope Benedict had built.

Divergent Reactions

I noticed too that in the broader Catholic world there began to be a split of sorts. Some of my Catholic friends were handling the situation by becoming liberal, rejecting the orthodox Catholic doctrines on moral issues and even on doctrinal ones.

Other friends went the other direction, becoming radical traditionalists who claimed the See of Peter was vacant, that there was no valid pope anymore. I watched with alarm as other friends became angry activists, protesting the Pope, the bishops, and anyone they perceived to be on the Pope Francis team.

These divisions were then exacerbated when the sexual abuse scandal broke out again in 2018. What most Catholics, myself included, assumed had been handled back in the early 2000s was found not to be the case. Rather, the actions of bad bishops and villainous priests were continuing to fester.

But none of my friends' different directions seemed right to me (although I understood the motivations behind them). I didn't want to become a heterodox liberal, or a radical traditionalist, or an angry activist, so after a short period of speaking up, by writing a blog post or two and posting to Facebook, and seeing my small voice drowned out by deafening roars on all sides, I went quiet.

I quit speaking up, even mildly, and instead silently pondered.

I mentally took note that every time that Pope Francis now said or wrote something, people from every side were making a hubbub, writing posts, yelling at each other, excoriating the pope, or defending him.

A small cottage industry developed among the Catholic world, fed like a gristmill on Pope Francis's latest words and actions.

I didn't want to have anything to do with the angry noise, so instead I turned inward, saw my own faults, and started working on myself. I also looked to my own family, my own community, to my circle of those around me whom I could actually have an influence on, and be influenced by.

There's a famous story where the great English author G.K. Chesterton was asked to write an editorial on the question of "What's wrong with the world?" He sent back his answer to the editor of the paper with only two words on it: "I am."

Similarly, I realized that the only person that I can directly change is myself. True, I can give a good witness to those around me by my virtuous actions, and occasionally I can say something directly to someone that may help them in their faith. And always, I can pray for people.

But the sole person I can improve is myself.

Secret Ingredients of the Saints

But I'm getting ahead of myself. By the time of Pope Francis's election, I had been Catholic for twelve years. In that time, I had read all about the saints, experienced some incredible things (both good and bad), and decided that I wanted to become a saint.

People use different language around becoming a saint. Some say, "grow in holiness," while others say "become the best version of yourself." I will use several of these phrases interchangeably.

In my search for how I could become the best version of myself, I discovered a new, old way to pray, one which all the saints had learned and practiced and become saints by doing. I will share what it is with you here in this book.

I learned how to overcome sins of lust, and grow strong in holy purity, by discovering other "secrets."

My wife and I ended up building a small group of other families around us, ones which have now become instrumental in our own faith, and with whom we have shared life in substantial ways.

Through trials, both metaphorical and literal, failures of many kinds, tragedy, pettiness, difficulties, and fears, God dropped breadcrumbs for me to follow, which I gathered up and combined into a recipe for holiness that each of the saints had long ago discovered.

I will share each of these "secret" ingredients with you in this book.

I keep putting "secret" in quotes, because, as you can probably guess, they aren't supposed to be secret at all. In fact, the Church has held them in her public treasure box for all to find for the past two thousand years.

But, like an old wooden chest belonging to your grandparents that sits up in the attic, the Church's treasure chest seems to have been largely forgotten by most Catholics--even by priests, bishops, and the pope--and so it sits gathering dust and cobwebs, waiting to be rediscovered by seeking souls who long to be nourished from the deep wellspring of the Church's Tradition.

Through suffering, trials, and difficulties over the course of 18 years, I unearthed the saintly ingredients and fit them together in a recipe. In doing so, I began to see a vision for what I could do personally to make a difference, the part that I could play in the Church and the world during this confusing time.

I began to see how I could fortify the Church from within and evangelize the world without.

What Is This Book About?

This book is a humble manifesto for how you can take action in a holy way during these dark times.

This book is a call to action on how *you* can make an impact for God.

God calls you to become a saint. You. A saint.

Becoming a saint has two facets: an inward one and an outward one.

Inwardly, you avail yourself of God's grace, conquer your faults and vices, and grow in virtue and prayer.

Outwardly, you take action that renews the Church and evangelizes the world.

This book is a collection of practical step-by-step plans, which you can do in your family, in your parish and diocese, and in your community to transform the world for Christ.

This book is for you if you are a committed Catholic, or want to be but have felt confused about what the right thing is to do when there seems to be so much error and conflict within the Church and persecution and craziness from society.

You may be thinking, "who is this guy that he thinks he can teach others to become saints?"

In this book I will share with you who I am, but I readily admit that everything I am going to share with you, you could find out for yourself.

The Church's writings and teachings are all there in the public domain: 2,000 years of tomes, lore, encyclicals, papal bulls, books, Councils, biographies, and histories.

You *could* start, as I did, with our Jewish roots at the beginning of recorded history and progress through the time of Christ and then on to the Apostolic Fathers, the pre- and post-Nicene Fathers, the first Ecumenical Councils, the Christological heresies, the Eastern Orthodox conflict, the Protestant schism, and so on down through the ages to today.

Such a study took me fifteen years.

You could then synthesize all that wisdom and figure out how to apply it to your own interior spiritual life, and outwardly to the Church and the world.

I've been working on doing that for a decade.

Or, you could take the direct path through the winding forest that I will show you. Let me guide you through the tangled wood, pointing out the valuable sights along the way, and you get to choose which ones God is calling you to focus on.

If this were a chef school, I've done the prep work for you in the kitchen. And now you can take the ingredients and work your culinary magic, magic only you can do.

What to Expect

In each of the following chapters, I will be sharing with you a real story from my own life. In each story I faced a serious problem, a problem that was solved only by discovering a secret that the saints practiced.

I will share each secret with you, so that you, too, can put it into practice in your own life and become a saint by following the secret recipe of the saints.

This is a journey, *the* journey, the only one worth going on. It will take all that you've got and all that you can give.

I'm ready to embark upon this journey.

Will you join me?

CHAPTER 2
Stalked By Anxiety

"Remember that you were at that time separated from
Christ, alienated from the commonwealth of Israel, and
strangers to the covenants of promise, having no hope and
without God in the world."
—Ephesians 2:12

I grew up on Nintendo and television.

My parents were both brought up in Christian homes, but by college they had abandoned whatever faith they had, so they reared my sister and me atheistically.

They phrased it differently than that of course: "We want you to choose for yourself what to think," was the actual line they used. But since we never prayed, never talked about God, never went to church, and since from an early age they taught us that we evolved from primordial ooze, unsurprisingly both my sister and I became just like our parents and rejected belief in God.

So by the time I reached junior high school, I had taken atheism to heart and began trying to convert my Christian friends away from their beliefs.

I recall playing video games with my Methodist school-mates and asking them why they believed in Jesus. As most other seventh graders would do, they looked at me in utter confusion, mumbled something vaguely about Jesus and their church, and we continued playing games.

In high school I set out to buttress my anti-faith even more, and chose evolution as the topic of my tenth grade research paper. I presented my paper to the class, showing all the scientific evidence for the claim that humans evolved from single-celled organisms. The thinly concealed payload of my report was the implication that believing in a god was ridiculous.

When my talk was finished, I took questions from my class about it. And I remember one classmate standing up, trembling with emotion, the quietest of my peers, who I had scarcely said five words to in all our years together in school.

With a voice quavering, not with fear, surprisingly, but with righteous anger, he said, "Jesus Christ saved me from suicide and I *know* He is real!" The room went uncomfortably silent, until our teacher hurriedly dispelled the tension by ending the question and answer session. What might have fazed a lesser atheist did not faze me. I shrugged it off with the thought, "if he's so weak as to need to believe in a magical deity to save him, that's his problem."

Inferno

The last project of my senior year was a book project, and my friend and I chose Dante's *Inferno*. This classic book takes the reader on a journey through Hell.

Our teacher afforded us quite a bit of creative license, so we crafted a papier-mâché, scale model of hell, complete with all the circles for the different sins people committed. For a personal touch, I stationed my Dungeons and Dragons figures along each circle to represent the demons who inflicted torment on the lost souls.

My friend and I laughed about the book's contents. To us, the torments of the Underworld were a fairy story no more real than *The Lord of the Rings* or other fantasy books we read.

Despite my cocky self-assurance, an uncomfortable thing happened during my class presentation of the Inferno project. While up at the front of the room explaining our project, I started to burn with heat, sweat beading on my brow. All eyes were on me. I feared that my classmates would see that I was sweating and that I would be humiliated. I wanted to run out of the room.

Fortunately, our presentation ended before any serious embarrassment could occur, but the whole situation was disconcerting to me.

I had never before experienced an anxiety about public humiliation. While it's not abnormal to have jitters about public speaking, and I had felt such nerves before, this was a whole new level of discomfort.

Little did I realize it was just the beginning.

College Atheism…And an Anxiety Disorder

High school graduation came, and off to Texas A&M University I went with my best friend, Nathan. I had a full scholarship and had applied to be a University Scholar as well.

A University Scholar was an honor only open to existing full scholarship holders, a kind of elitist's elite, given to just fifteen students in each class. Texas A&M is a huge school, so this was a prestigious award.

I interviewed and impressed the panel with my urbanity and self-deprecation, most of which was falsely modest garbage. I became a University Scholar. But the problem was that every University Scholar had to act as an ambassador of the university and that meant doing regular public speaking.

With every talk, my anxiety increased. My stomach would become unsettled as the day of the talk got closer, then while presenting, my body temperature would rise, and I would visibly perspire. Nausea would break over me in waves. I found ways of dodging as many of these ambassador events as I could.

Soon, however, these anxieties began to spread into other areas of my life. In fact, any social situation. Sitting in a classroom during a lecture, eating dinner with friends, going out to a bar—anything where I was around others—became an occasion for anxiety to take hold. Nausea would wash over me; I'd start sweating and soon have to leave the room on the pretense of using the restroom.

Fear became my constant companion. Fear of enduring humiliation in front of others and fear of their disgust if they found out I had these problems. A vicious cycle formed, where the anxious feelings would manifest in embarrassing ways. I felt helpless to break the cycle, serving to increase my anxiety even more for next time.

No one knew that anything was wrong with me. I hid it well. But the strain of maintaining a pleasant façade while my life crumbled intensified as each week passed.

Rocket Science and Anxiety

I was now a junior, studying electrical engineering, and I was accepted into the internship program at NASA Johnson Space Center in Houston. I met the other interns and knew that they planned social activities, but I avoided going to any of them, fearing more anxiety attacks.

I worked on my intern project and tried to avoid as many meetings with my team as I could. I even asked one of my older coworkers to give my project's presentation at the end of the semester, so I could avoid speaking in public.

One day I was sitting in the cafeteria alone and overheard a fellow intern say, "Look over there: it's 'Anti'; he doesn't do anything with us." I knew intuitively that "Anti" meant anti-social. Wow, here I was, a young man who had never lacked friends, who had always gotten along with others, being talked of as a weird loner.

That day the anxieties became particularly bad, and when I went home, the fears spiraled out of control. Cascade after cascade of panicked thoughts shoved their way into my consciousness. I tried to put them away but couldn't. They were too strong.

One fed into another and then back around, a self-perpetuating cycle of anxiety. Panicked thoughts raced around my mind: "I'm going to have to quit school, and I'll never finish my degree, and I'll have to live with my mom or be a bum on the streets, because I won't be able to work, so I'll never have a wife or a good life."

My head pounded. My stomach roiled, and I went to the bathroom, staring at myself in the mirror. Instead of just seeing my reflection, I seemed to be looking at myself from a higher angle, a kind of third-person disconnection from my body.

"What is happening to me? What is happening!" I said to myself. "Am I having a nervous breakdown? I just want to be happy and not have these problems!"

After thirty minutes of this terror, the panic subsided. I thought for sure this was what people meant by having a nervous breakdown. I had hidden these anxieties from everyone. I was self-reliant and thought that I needed no one but myself.

"These problems are just chemical imbalances in my brain," I told myself. I would use sheer willpower to correct them. But after years of daily dread, I knew it wasn't true. I needed help.

With nothing left to lose, I decided to tell my mother about my anxiety problem.

Psychological Therapy

My mother was very concerned about me and patiently listened to me recount years of living with this pain. She found a psychologist for me, and to my great relief I learned that there was a name for my problems. I had depression and social anxiety with a panic disorder. Beautiful! Never before had I been so excited to be diagnosed.

Eagerly I asked the psychologist, "Okay, so where's the pill that I take to make this better?"

"There is no pill that takes this all away," she said.

Nonetheless, she prescribed me an anti-anxiety medication to help, and I started on a program of cognitive behavioral therapy, which consisted of breathing exercises, positive thinking routines, and other intellectual and physical tactics to try to control the fears. I embarked on this regimen with gusto, optimistic that my problems would soon lessen.

But they didn't lessen. They continued getting worse. The pills and therapy weren't working, even after months of trying. I was in trouble, and began to finally despair. My own mental tricks hadn't worked; professional help wasn't working. Medication did little. Life was filled with constant dread, and death started to look inviting.

Driving home from one of the last days of my internship at NASA, I watched the cars from oncoming traffic whiz past me, hoping that one would accidentally swerve into my lane and end my life. I was too afraid to take my own life, but if someone else ended it for me, leaving my obituary without the shame of suicide, I would have embraced it.

A Biblical Life Raft

In my desperation to try anything, my thoughts turned to a group of friends back at A&M, all Christians. One of these friends, named Steven was also an engineering major and had befriended me.

I had always thought Christianity was stupid and that Christians were deluded. I saw no reason to believe in God, and I had debated with these Christian friends many times. Now, however, I wasn't thinking of debating them. I thought instead of how much peace I knew they had. Not a fake peace or plastic happiness, but a deep contentment and joy that was evident in their lives.

I had on my bookshelf an old King James Bible, given to me by my cousins when I was ten years old. Though I was a militant atheist, I had always kept this Bible—even an atheist thinks twice before trashing one.

That night, I dusted it off and began reading. I also tossed up the first prayer of my life to the God I didn't believe in: "Lord, supposedly this book is your word. I don't believe in you, but I am in trouble and need help. If you are real, help me."

If God was trying to write me a love letter—something I had heard Christians say about their Scriptures—the Bible was an odd way to do it.

I began in Genesis. It started innocuously enough: world is created; people are made; they disobey God and get kicked out of the garden. But from there, things seemed to just get really strange, with this person begetting that person, the Tower of Babel, people living for hundreds of years, big flood killing almost everyone. It was almost like you needed a guide to the Bible to make sense of any of it. My King James version didn't have that, and to make matters worse, the language was full of thees and thous. Some love letter this was.

I was not surprised that after one week of saying a short prayer each evening and reading the Bible, I felt no diminishing of my anxieties at all. I was a practical guy though. I'd spent twenty years as a devout atheist, so I could at least give God one month.

I didn't know what faith was and wondered how to gain it. I knew it wasn't something that I could manufacture. Some people seemed born with it, or at least they received it early on from their parents. Unlike them, I'd received atheism from my parents. We never said even one prayer growing up. Faith may as well have been on Mars.

One thing was certain: God was my last shot. Each of the methods that I had tried before had been fruitless. My anxiety disorder just kept getting worse. Panic attacks became frequent, terrifying occurrences, and I realized that agoraphobia—an intense fear of having a panic attack in a place where you cannot escape—had also begun to take hold of me.

So here I was, on my knees. God either existed and would choose to do something to help me, or He didn't exist, and I would receive no help and die.

But something noticeable happened during the second week of Bible reading and praying. I was still in the first two books, where strange people with even stranger names were having children, fighting battles, and being turned into pillars of salt.

I noticed that my fears had lessened by a small amount. Not daring to get excited, since I figured random fluctuations could have caused the improvement, I soldiered on with reading and praying. The whole exercise of prayer was still so foreign, and my self-consciousness at the fact that I was doing it still so great, that I kept my prayers brief. "If God is God," I thought. "Then he doesn't need me to go on and on about my problems."

The third week continued, and I felt a twinge of something that could almost be described as the precursor to the introduction to the beginnings of faith. It gave me a little hope that maybe this was working. Whether "this" was Jesus or just some temporary placebo effect of prayer, I couldn't yet say. Only time would tell.

And it did. I plowed through book after book of the Bible, reading ten chapters a day, skimming through parts that I did not understand. The Bible is long, and I figured that if God wanted to tell me something important, He would put information in multiple places for redundancy's sake. Throughout these weeks, my fears slowly lessened. Also inexplicably, I sensed a tiny amount of faith growing in me.

My internship mercifully ended, and I went back to school for the summer session. One of my Christian friends, Bryan, was sticking around, so we roomed together. I told him that I was reading the Bible. I wasn't willing to tell him about my anxieties yet, but I wanted him to know that I was checking the whole Christianity thing out.

He must have been secretly thrilled, and no doubt had been praying for me for a long time, because a few days later he bought me a Bible—New International Version (NIV)—that was in modern English and had helpful study notes all over the place, presumably in an attempt to help bewildered readers like me makes sense of it.

An Atheist Goes to Church

Bryan invited me to go to church with him, and I reluctantly agreed, secretly dreading that I would have to sit in the middle of a pew with no way to easily get out in case I had a panic attack.

I had read enough of the Bible, however, to know that Jesus had started a Church and that Baptists were somehow part of it, so I resolved to check it out. I sat at the end of the pew, near the exit, planning for an escape should the need arise.

The service began and everyone stood to sing. I knew none of the songs, having never experienced "praise and worship" music before. Then the pastor got up and gave the sermon.

It seemed to me that during that whole half hour he spoke, he only covered three verses, and they were all from the New Testament. I was still in the Old one, so this intrigued me. At the end of the service, the pastor told everyone to bow their heads and pray, and he started talking. He told the congregation that anyone who wanted to put their trust in Jesus should come forward right then and there, in what I now know is called an "altar call." Maybe Bryan hoped I would go forward, but there wasn't a chance of that.

It was enough for me that I survived going to church for the first time.

Summer of the Sinner's Prayer

That summer, I continued reading the Bible and praying as well as talking to Bryan about Christianity. He wasn't an expert, but he certainly knew a lot more about Jesus and the Bible than I did. By the end of the summer, I had almost finished the entire Bible with Bryan's help.

I didn't know it at the time, but I had providentially stumbled across the first ingredient in the recipe of the saints: the Bible.

Many years later, I would discover how much the saints valued the Bible. St. Josemaria Escriva said "God has called us Catholics to follow him closely. In that holy Writing you will find the Life of Jesus, but you should also find your own life there."

I was beginning to find my own life in the Bible, and it amazed me.

From listening to the pastor of the Baptist church, I learned that we are sinners and need Jesus for forgiveness and salvation. I also learned that the official way to obtain this forgiveness was by praying a certain kind of prayer, admitting to Christ that I was a sinner and asking for forgiveness. Then He would enter my heart and be my savior. My pastor explained that while "the sinner's prayer" was not in the Bible verbatim, if you stitched a few verses together you could come up with something like it.

Finally, I was ready, and one night I prayed the sinner's prayer. I confessed to God that I was a sinner in need of Christ's mercy. I asked Him to come into my heart right then and there. I felt a little better after doing it, but I wasn't quite sure that anything had really changed. My faith was still slowly growing. I was learning more about God. I was going to church.

In my heart I envisioned a little sapling of faith growing in a small clearing within a dark forest. That sapling was my newfound faith, but it was frail, and all the doubts and darkness I was living in threatened to crush it utterly.

I knew I had to protect that sapling and give it a chance to grow. My old way of living had not worked. This was do-or-die.

That fall semester, all my Christian friends returned to school, and we started doing Bible studies together. My friends explained things to me about God, faith, the Bible, and salvation.

During this time, faith finally overwhelmed my doubts. The floodgates of faith opened up. What I had failed to do through my own mental efforts and psychological tactics, God has done through supernatural grace. My anxieties diminished substantially for the first time ever.

I couldn't get enough of reading the Bible and talking to my Christian friends about my newfound discoveries. They were thrilled, especially since I used to be their theological enemy.

Floodgates of Faith

My last year at A&M centered around our Baptist church. I volunteered with the church youth group to help out poor kids in the bad part of town; we put on a camp for them and many of them "got saved" by the end of it.

On Sundays, my friends and I first went to the regular church service and then to Sunday school and then to another praise and worship music service after that. We did a Bible study every week and read Christian books together.

Eventually, I felt a strong desire to get baptized. I believed that it was biblical, a public proclamation that I had put my trust in Jesus. So, the following Sunday I positioned myself in just the right pew to make for an easy walk to the altar.

And when the time for the altar call came that Sunday, with everyone bowing their heads in prayer, I went up to the front and told the pastor I wanted to be baptized. He announced it to the congregation and everyone cheered.

A few weeks later I was baptized by the youth minister, full immersion, in front of the whole church. I was petrified by anxieties before walking out into the baptismal pool inside the church, but Jesus had commanded that His followers do this, so I knew I had to.

My parents were both there which meant a lot to me. My dad later informed me that he was okay with my faith because he also had "found religion in college." Given how he had brought me up, with no faith at all, I wasn't sure what he meant by that, but I understood that he meant well.

My life now dramatically improved. God's grace, through reading the Bible and praying, was working inside me. My anxieties continued to decline. I had hope for a good life again and for an eternal future of love. Jesus was my friend and brother and Lord. The Holy Spirit was inside me, bearing His fruit and giving me His gifts. And God the Father loved me.

I was now a new creation in Christ. The old was gone; the new had come (2 Corinthians 5:17).

I had turned to God to escape from my crippling anxieties. But God had other plans: to use those anxieties to lead me to rebirth and truth.

I was a happy Baptist now, going to church and having fellowship with my Christian friends. I learned every week from my pastor's sermons and continued doing Bible studies. All that was left for my life to be complete, I thought, was to meet a pretty young Baptist woman, get married, and live happily ever after.

There was only one problem: I had a Catholic friend named Gerardo. And he had other plans, which I'll share with you in this next chapter.

How to Mix in This Ingredient

The Bible is a thick set of books, all inspired by God, that we Catholics want to read and understand.

But it is not easy to do so: its length, scope, breadth, and content are daunting, even to scholars. So how can we as regular Catholics approach it?

Which Bible to Read?

To begin with, you want to buy a good Bible, by which I mean a Catholic Bible (so it has *all* the books God inspired, unlike the Protestant one), with an accurate translation, and orthodox study notes.

Those criteria narrow down the options to only a handful. I recommend either the Ignatius Study Bible or the Didache Study Bible. Both use the same solid translation: the Revised Standard Version, 2nd Catholic Edition, and both have orthodox study notes and helpful explanatory articles included.

How to Read the Bible?

You can tackle reading the Bible from many angles, but I am going to recommend a few.

Most people find it helpful to follow some sort of guide to reading the Bible within a given timeframe. For instance, multiple guides exist to help you read the Bible in a year. I recommend getting the guide from The Coming Home Network[1] and using it to read the Bible in a year.

Using a guide like this keeps you on track to read the whole Bible in a year, which is quite an accomplishment. The study notes in the Bibles I recommended will help you understand what you are reading, not perfectly, but over time you will get a better and better feel for what the Scriptures mean.

---

1   https://chnetwork.org/free-resource-updated-version-of-our-read-the-bible-and-the-catechism-in-a-year-guide/

Also, I encourage you to take a long term view on reading the Scriptures. They should be a lifelong study and source for reflection. Over time, your understanding of the Bible, and thus of our Lord's wisdom, will grow.

The Recipe of the Saints

(At the end of each chapter, I will include the running list of ingredients in the recipe of the saints as I found them.)

First ingredient: The Bible

CHAPTER 3

Unity in the Truth

"The glory which thou hast given me I have given to them,
that they may be one even as we are one, I in them and
thou in me, that they may become perfectly one, so that
the world may know that thou hast sent me and hast loved
them even as thou hast loved me."
—John 17:22,23

Becoming a Christian was the greatest thing that had happened to me.

I was going to church and doing Bible studies, being "discipled" by a Christian grandfather I looked up to, and growing in friendship with my newfound Christian brothers. To top it off, my anxieties continued to lessen and lose their death grip on me.

During this time of discovery and healing, I went to the Christian bookstore and found a book by Max Lucado called *Just Like Jesus*. On the back cover, I read these fascinating words: "God loves you just way you are, but he refuses to leave you there. He wants you to be just like Jesus."

That is what I wanted to be! Just like Jesus. And I was learning how to do that by reading the Bible, but also I knew

I needed to learn from wise Christians like Max Lucado who were further along in their walk with God.

I took the book home to my college apartment and devoured it. Lucado wove stories of people's lives, broken and wounded, but whom Jesus encountered and transformed. By following Jesus, they went from hatred to forgiveness, sin to repentance, egotistical pride to humility.

This is how I wanted to be, so I started intentionally striving each day to live as I thought Jesus would live. I wanted to know fully what Jesus taught and understand it, so I could follow Him.

The only problem was: how was I supposed to interpret Jesus' words accurately so that I knew how to follow Him?

Dominated By Denominations

In my short time as a Baptist, I had already encountered divisions within Christianity.

Why were we Christians so divided? Our Southern Baptist teachings differed from those of other denominations, and we certainly didn't worship with them: they had their church, and we had ours.

Our very large Baptist church was only a block away from a large Presbyterian one, reminding me on a weekly basis of these divisions. Driving to church one Sunday morning, I asked my Protestant roommate: "What do they believe at that Presbyterian church?" He admitted that he didn't know.

This began a long series of discussions that I had with my roommates about the lack of Christian unity and whether it was a problem. John 17 indicated that Jesus wanted us to be unified as one. This issue got me thinking about what I believed and, more importantly, *why* I believed it.

I had only been a believer for a year and had only been baptized for a few months, but already I subscribed to the Southern Baptist teachings and had rejected, for example, many of the Catholic Church's teachings. How had I, a newly minted Christian, come so quickly to the conclusions about which denomination taught the fullest and most accurate truth?

I realized then that I had been influenced strongly when becoming a Christian by my Evangelical friends. As an atheist, I "knew" on some level that there were many different kinds of Christians and vaguely understood that they differed in some beliefs, but to me at that time, they were all about the same.

I recalled that during my conversion from atheism, I often didn't understand what I was reading in the Bible. I would look down in the NIV Bible's study notes section and see if there was an explanation about the verse, and usually there was; it was very helpful, I thought. But I didn't realize that Protestant theologians of a certain "slant" had written all these explanatory notes to support their specific interpretive opinions.

Also, when I had questions about the faith, I would ask my Baptist friends, and they would answer me according to what they believed was true. Similarly, I went to the church they went to, Central Baptist, and I listened to the pastor there expound upon the Bible and explain what the true Christian teachings were as he understood them. I realized that I had chosen the Evangelical Protestant understanding of the Christian Faith without deliberately giving other denominations a chance.

And so I returned to my intention to become like Jesus with a new zeal to know which denomination's teachings were closest to the truth that God revealed. I prayed fervently that Jesus would guide me because I wanted to be as close to Him as possible.

Since the Bible is the inerrant word of God, I assumed that if everyone just read the Bible and asked God for guidance, they would all come to the one truth that He intended. But two thousand years of Christian divisions said otherwise. If the Bible is all we have to go on, yet it doesn't result in unity, how can we know divine truth with certainty?

While I didn't know the answer yet, I felt confident that God would reveal the solution to me.

About That Catholic Friend

In a sea of Protestant friends, I had one Catholic friend, named Gerardo. Rather I should say I had one Catholic friend who practiced his faith.

I had lots of Catholic friends who lived about like I had lived as an atheist. They weren't very good marketing agents for Catholicism and in fact confirmed my Baptist biases that the Catholic Church wasn't a true Christian faith.

But Gerardo was different: he was a practicing Catholic, and, most perplexingly, he really seemed to believe in Jesus. Like my Baptist friends, he was thrilled that I had left atheism and embraced faith in God. He was less thrilled, however, with my choice to become a Baptist, especially since he felt I hadn't given Roman Catholicism a fair shot.

And he was right: I had not spent three years gathering together all evidence for and against each different Christian group, weighing them on the scales and making a scientific decision, because it is simply not possible to do so.

Catholicism's Challenge

Gerardo and I went to lunch one afternoon, and he spent the time trying to tease out the differences in our beliefs and show me that the Catholic Church was true. I didn't buy it.

For instance, I pointed out that the Catholic Church believed that Mary was sinless, but the Bible said that all had sinned. Case closed. Obvious contradiction. I had many other objections, from bishops and popes and priests to rituals and weird customs, but the Mary stuff was more than enough to discount Catholicism right out of the gate.

But Gerardo didn't give up. The next time we met, he pointed to my Bible and said: "How do you know that that is the exact set of books that God inspired, no more and no less?" Now, this was a tricky question, and I had never really thought about it before. I had read a bit about the Bible, how well it fit together, how one book reinforced and even fulfilled another, how they quoted each other, and so on.

But I didn't have a full defense of the Protestant *canon* (as the set of books is called). I was confident that I would find a compelling answer, because every time my new faith had been challenged so far, I researched and discovered solid answers.

I had no fear that this would not be the case with the canon of Scripture. So I told Gerardo that I would get back with him. I went home to my apartment and began searching. I asked my Protestant friends: "Why do Catholics have seven books that we don't?"

They answered in various ways: "Those extra Catholic books were added in the sixteenth century. They contain obvious falsehoods, historical errors, and myths in them. Evil things are condoned in them."

That sounded good, but coming from atheism and reading the entire (Protestant) Bible from cover to cover multiple times, I had also run into certain (apparent) contradictions, errors, and myths—all in the sixty-six books Protestants claim are the only inspired ones. Further, from my research I discovered that "those extra Catholic books" were *not* added in the sixteenth century but had been in the Bible since the early Church.

Undeterred, I went online, did a search, and started reading some of the more popular Protestant apologetics blogs. (Apologetics means that you defend a particular set of beliefs using logical reasoning, so apologetics for a Protestant is where they try to defend Protestantism's teachings.) The internet had really taken off while I was in college, and by this time just about anything could be found online.

I read the Protestant arguments for the canon, but I also found the Catholic arguments for theirs. And they both seemed cogent to me. I could see how either one could be true. Worse, I encountered a passage in one of the seven Catholic books that smacked of pure Christological prophecy (Wisdom, chapter 2). Sure, a blind squirrel finds an acorn every once in a while, but these verses were too accurate to be lucky guesses.

Adoration

I wanted to study the subject of the canon more, and I found a way to do so in an unexpected place. My friend Gerardo kept telling me about something called "Adoration." He was regularly "going to Adoration," so eventually I asked him what it was.

He explained that Catholics, believing that Jesus is truly present in the consecrated Host in Holy Communion, place this Host in a golden container and display it for Catholics to adore.

It seemed more than a little strange to me, but I had to agree it was consistent with Catholic beliefs. If I believed Jesus was present somewhere on the planet, I would go there immediately, kneel before Him, and worship Him.

I decided to give it a try. I asked Gerardo when this Adoration took place, and where. The next day, I was at the entrance to the Catholic student center. I didn't know the Catholic protocols and gestures and feared that a Catholic, especially a priest, might spot me and immediately recognize that I was not Catholic and tell me to leave.

I saw a young woman open the door and walk in, and I tailed in after her nonchalantly. She dipped her hand in the holy water bowl and made the Sign of the Cross. I wasn't ready to do that, so I moseyed around to the side and back of the room, observing what the people were doing.

There were about ten people in the room, all kneeling or sitting. Some had their eyes closed; others were reading. All were silent. At the front of the room on a table was a golden *something* with circular glass in the middle of it. It looked like a statue of a sun with golden rays of metal fanning out from the center.

"That must be it," I thought. I sat down on a chair and in my heart asked our Lord that if He were really present that He would show me. I didn't know what might happen: something miraculous? Or maybe just an interior nudge that God would use to help me understand.

I was afraid of committing the sin of idolatry and worshiping a created thing instead of God, so He was going to have to make it clear that I was not doing that.

For the next thirty minutes, I prayed, read my Bible, and felt a great peace descend upon me, almost a drowsy feeling. I didn't know if that answered my question, but it seemed to be all I would get. I got up and quietly went out of the room.

Unwittingly, I had just discovered one of the secret ingredients of the saints, Eucharistic Adoration.

St. Alphonsus Liguori wrote of Jesus in the Blessed Sacrament: "Good friends find pleasure in one another's company.

Let us know pleasure in the company of our best Friend, a Friend who can do everything for us, a friend who loves us beyond measure. Here in the Blessed Sacrament we can talk to him straight from the heart."

I had just had my first such conversation, straight from my heart, in the close company of my best Friend. I would have many more conversations in Adoration in the coming years, and my "Holy Hour" would grow to become one of my favorite things about being Catholic. Later, I would learn that many of the saints sat everyday for hours before our Lord in Adoration.

I started going to Adoration about once a week. And during those times, I read about how the books of the Bible were chosen and why Catholic and Protestant Bibles differed in size.

As a Protestant, I believed that God had inspired sixty-six books to be written, and this was the sole infallible rule of our faith. But Protestants didn't believe that God had protected any other discernment in the early Church from error.

So I searched for the reason to believe that God had only protected the Church from error in discerning the canon of Scripture, yet permitted His Church to fall into corruption regarding baptism, the Eucharist, the priesthood, the veneration of the saints, the Mass, and so on.

If God only inspired those books to be written but then didn't guide someone else to know that those were the right books, we were still up a creek. We needed a "sixty-seventh" infallible action by God that would point to the sixty-six books and say: "*Those* are the inspired ones, people!"

Unfortunately, the history of the canon's discernment was anything but that simple and obvious. Christians over the course of three hundred years proposed lists of books, debated and argued about them, while slowly the true canon crystallized.

Did God protect those men from error? My Protestant faith answered "no," because I had been taught that the Church had fallen into error by the second or third century. In fact, there was no reason to think that the canon had God's special protection from error at all. And if we couldn't know which books made up the Bible with certainty, our entire Christian Faith was built on a shaky foundation.

I was already biased strongly toward Protestantism, but I hadn't been one long enough to not see that a big, arbitrary leap was at the root of my newly found beliefs. That didn't sit well with me. During Adoration I brought this dilemma to Jesus and asked Him to help me resolve it.

Catechism

Around this time, Gerardo gave me a Catechism of the Catholic Church. This book, he explained, was a "summary of all Catholic teaching."

"Some summary," I thought as I hefted the book. It must have been 500 pages long!

Since I was now unsure that the Bible alone was the sole infallible rule of faith, I read the Catechism with interest. Each paragraph explained some part of Catholic teaching, often citing Bible verses, but also quotes from the saints, from popes, and from various Councils the Catholic Church had held over the centuries.

In the Catechism, I was introduced to the idea of sacred Tradition, of which the Scriptures formed an integral part. It was not the Scriptures *alone* that contained God's divine revelation, but the Scriptures together with the Tradition of the Church. This Tradition was a living thing, like a stream of water flowing through time within the Church, with Christ as its source, and the Holy Spirit as its flow. In fact, the way that Catholics knew which books belonged in the Bible was through the Church's Tradition! Catholicism did not have the same problem at its root that Protestantism did.

In reading the Catechism, I encountered quote after quote by different saints explaining the teachings of the Catholic Church over the past 2,000 years. The Catholic Faith now made even more sense to me, because the Catechism logically connected one doctrine to another and explained from the Bible and from the teachings of the early Church where each belief came from.

I learned that the Church had published many Catechisms over the centuries, in various languages, for different audiences, both laity and clergy (priests and bishops). St. Robert Bellarmine, himself one of the great defenders of the Faith, even wrote a Catechism himself four hundred years ago that was in the form of a dialogue for easy understanding.

So it was that I found another secret ingredient of the saints: the deposit of faith summarized eloquently in the Catechism. It would take me many years to fully appreciate what I had discovered.

Over the next four months, I read the entire Catechism, and though I didn't believe all that I encountered in it, I knew I had to take the next step.

The Catholic Church It Is

I could no longer remain outside the Catholic Church, so in my last semester of college, I started the classes to become Catholic. I now knew that the Church was the beacon of hope and truth in a world of darkness and despair.

The Church was ancient and true, guided by the Spirit of God, full of beauty and wonder. It was the fulfillment of my Protestant beliefs, perfecting them and putting them in their proper context. The Bible opened up through the light of the Apostolic Tradition. I met Jesus at the Mass and got to know Him like I never had before.

Not satisfied that I had found only part of the truth, God led me into its fullness in the Catholic Church. All my Protestant friends ultimately ended our friendship. They were happy with me as their convert to Protestant Christianity; they felt betrayed by me as the Catholic apostate.

It hurt, but I had discovered something so beautiful and deep that it more than compensated for the loss of their friendship. My allegiance was to Jesus, and not to man.

The Journey Had Just Begun

Becoming Catholic was the end of one journey, but the beginning of an even greater one. The beginning of *the* journey, the one I am still on now, almost twenty years later. I didn't realize it at the time, but God was now going to start working on me in earnest, and it would be difficult, painful, confusing, wondrous, illuminating, and thrilling.

The lessons I learned have transformed my life. But not without trials, beginning with the most fundamental decision of what God wanted me to do with my life, which I will share with you in the next chapter.

How to Mix in This Ingredient

I had discovered Eucharistic Adoration and the Catechism of the Catholic Church, two ingredients the saints took part in. Here is how you can incorporate them into your life of faith.

Eucharistic Adoration

You can adore our Lord in the Eucharist in multiple settings: at any Catholic Church with a tabernacle (Jesus in the Blessed Sacrament is reposed within), at an Adoration chapel where the Blessed Sacrament is exposed in a monstrance, or even at Holy Mass when our Lord becomes really present in the consecration.

I recommend that you first "give it a try" by finding an Adoration chapel at a Catholic Church in your area, and simply visiting it, quietly praying before the Blessed Sacrament, for as long as you like.

After getting the feel for Adoration, I would look around the chapel entrance, where typically there is a registry or log book of people going to Adoration, which the coordinators use to ensure that there is always at least one person adoring Jesus, that He is not left alone.

Look for a sign up sheet or for the contact information for the coordinators, and then choose an hour on a day of the week that generally works well for you, and sign up for that hour. It is called your "Holy Hour" because every week you will go to the chapel and adore Jesus there.

This hour affords you the perfect time for reading the Scriptures, praying (which I'll share more with you about later on in the book), and for reading the Catechism as well.

Catechism

The Catechism, like the Bible, is a thick book. But unlike the Bible, it has been broken up into short paragraphs on given topics, and those topics have been categorized together in an orderly way, with the goal of summarizing the teachings of the Catholic Church.

The Catechism is a sure guide to what the Catholic Church teaches, and thus it is a wellspring of knowledge to help you understand the Faith.

In the previous chapter, I recommended a guide for reading the Bible; the same exists for the Catechism[2]. You could use the guide, or, alternately, you could simply start reading the Catechism from cover-to-cover, a practice which is generally discouraged in regard to the Bible, since it makes the Bible harder to grasp.

Understanding the Faith will help you to become a better Catholic, and also will equip you to defend your beliefs when they are challenged (which in our day and age, is a certainty).

The Catechism often cites Scripture verses, which you can then find in your Bible, as well as Church documents like the writings of the popes and Church Councils.

---

2   https://chnetwork.org/free-resource-updated-version-of-our-read-the-bible-and-the-catechism-in-a-year-guide/

The Recipe of the Saints

The Bible
Eucharistic Adoration
Catechism of the Catholic Church

CHAPTER 4

Called to the Priesthood?

"The Lord has sworn and will not change his mind, 'You
are a priest forever after the order of Melchiz'edek.'"
—Psalm 110:4

I was a new Catholic and very happy. I was single, had recently
graduated college, and had started my first job in my new
career.

Shortly after becoming Catholic, I encountered St. Francis
of Assisi. Even as an atheist, I had heard of St. Francis, but now,
as a Catholic, I began to learn more deeply about how he actually lived his life.

I learned that he practiced extreme poverty and made vows
of chastity and obedience. At the time, I could not imagine a
more radical way of following Jesus than these.

What if God was calling me to such a radical way of life as
well, to religious life or to the priesthood?

I wanted to follow wherever God led me, but I was still not
completely healed of all my anxieties. Being a priest meant you
had to be in the spotlight, with all eyes on you, and I wondered
whether I could ever do that.

I also had a fear that God "had it in for me." Would He call me to do the very thing I most dreaded, just as He had called me to become Catholic when it was something that I had despised? He seemed to have plans that were quite different from how I imagined my life to go, and I wondered with trepidation if He would call me to be a priest, in spite of my anxieties about it.

I wasn't sure of the answer yet, so I just kept praying. I had been asking God what He wanted me to do with my life. Did He want me to become a priest? But month after month, I got no response and started to feel frustrated. "Why won't you speak to me Lord? This is something so important and vital to my whole life!" I shouted from my heart.

Yet God remained silent.

The Rosary Reveals My Next Step

A few months prior, right at the end of college when I was entering the Catholic Church, a friend gave me a book by St. Louis De Montfort called *The Secret of the Rosary*. I didn't know much about the Rosary, and as a former Protestant, I had been on guard against Mary in particular, since I'd been taught that Catholics worship Mary.

In becoming Catholic, I realized that Catholics did not worship Mary and that it was okay to seek her intercession, but old prejudices die hard, and I still felt uncomfortable about it. Further, I was still living with my three Protestant roommates. They knew I was becoming Catholic, and they deeply opposed my decision. So I was afraid of praying the Rosary where they could hear me or find out.

In spite of my reservations, God kept bringing to my attention things that demanded I learn about the Rosary. So I did some research. I learned that our Lady personally gave

St. Dominic the Rosary, instructing him on how it should be prayed. St. Dominic would later say, "One day, through the Rosary...Our Lady will save the world."

That was enough for me to take the next step, in spite of my old Protestant biases. I decided to open up *The Secret of the Rosary*, and I read it. In doing so, I realized that I needed to ask our Lady to pray for me in the Rosary, to obtain the graces that I needed to discern whether God was calling me to the priesthood.

So one day, when all my Protestant roommates were out of the house, I pulled out the one rosary I owned, a gift from my friend Gerardo, the same one who had helped me discover the Catholic Church. I went into the bedroom I shared with my three friends, went under the covers of my bed, and quietly started to pray.

It felt odd, saying these prayers to Mary. And I had to keep referring back to the pamphlet I had picked up that explained how to pray the Rosary. Fearing that my roommates would barge into the apartment and discover me, my heart was beating fast. If they found me praying to Mary, I didn't know what they might do.

Twenty minutes later, I completed the final prayer and made the Sign of the Cross. Shortly after, my roommates returned to the apartment. Whew!

I kept reading more on the Rosary. Every bit I learned confirmed how powerful it was.

St. Louis de Montfort described it this way: "If you say the Rosary faithfully until death, I assure you that in spite of the gravity of your sins, you shall receive a never-fading crown of glory. Even if you are on the brink of damnation, even if you have one foot in Hell, even if you have sold your soul to the devil as sorcerers do who practice black magic, and even if you are a heretic as obstinate as a devil, sooner or later you will be converted and will amend your life and save your soul, if, and mark well what I say--if you say the Holy Rosary devoutly every day until death for the purpose of knowing the truth and obtaining contrition and pardon of your sins."

Incredible. If devout praying of the Rosary can save souls on the brink of damnation, surely God would direct me in my discernment of the priesthood?

Praying the Rosary felt awkward for the first month, but I stuck with it. I kept praying the Rosary on a regular basis, and through it, I received the grace to know what the next step if I should take was.

A Retreat Surprise

Through the Rosary, I realized that I could not just *think* about the priesthood and religious life in the abstract. I needed to actually meet priests and religious brothers and sisters, talk to them, and see whether I could imagine myself as a priest.

I started by going on our diocesan discernment retreat. Many young men and women who were thinking about the priesthood and religious life attended, as well as representatives from several religious Orders, including nuns and priests, as well as priests of our diocese.

At this retreat many religious men and women gave talks, and they held discussion sessions where you could talk directly to the priests and nuns and learn about the religious life.

One priest was from the Paulist religious community, the order in charge of the local university Catholic student center. I asked if he would like to go for a walk with me on the retreat grounds, and he happily agreed.

While on the walk, I asked him about his community, what their unique charism was (the special way that they followed Jesus), as well as what it was like for him to be a priest at the college.

To my shock, in his responses he started using profanity. He was dropping curse words left and right as he described his experiences as a priest. I think that this was his effort to try to "be cool" and relate with me, but he couldn't have been further off the mark.

The next day of the retreat we got to sit down together in a group of young people and talk to a nun. This nun, the first I had ever met, surprised me, because I noticed that she was not wearing a habit, the customary garb that I had always associated with nuns, at least from old pictures and movies.

During our discussion, I said something about how some men are called to the priesthood, and she interrupted me and gave me a funny look. She then took on a patronizing tone in her voice, as if she were instructing a small, ignorant child, and she explained to me how "women were going to soon be priests," and that the Catholic Church was finally "getting with the times."

I was speechless, but the last thing I wanted to do was to argue with a nun, who I assumed was much holier than I and certainly knew the Catholic Faith better, having lived it her whole life. I asked a clarifying question because I thought perhaps I had misunderstood what she said, but she reiterated emphatically that women could also be priests and that this would happen one day soon.

I didn't say anything more. (Perhaps I should have spoken up, but I was not confident enough in my Catholic faith yet to challenge a nun.) Instead, all the rest of that day at the retreat,

I questioned my beliefs and assumptions on what it meant to be a priest.

In spite of these discouraging interactions, the next day I was able to spend a lot of time in prayer, talking with God about what He desired for me. I mentally separated what these priests and religious said from what I knew the Church taught and did not let it disturb me from considering a vocation to the priesthood.

That retreat ended, and I began to think about specific religious communities that I might be called too. Since St. Therese of Lisieux was my Confirmation saint, I began exploring the Carmelite religious Order.

The Carmelite house nearest me was having a "Come and See" retreat weekend, so I signed up and went, eager to meet real Carmelites and see how they followed our Lord.

With the Carmelites

I was with a small group of other young men, and for the weekend we were led by two Carmelite seminarians. We listened to various talks by the Carmelite priests, but I was perplexed by the irreverent tone they used, including by the very priest who was the vocation director as he described their daily life.

Later that evening, we went out into the city with the two seminarians, who were going to show us around the area. As we were walking through the city, one of them pointed out a strip club and asked whether we wanted to go inside.

I said, "Are you joking?" He laughed and said "well I guess not, huh?" and we kept on walking.

Imagine a seminarian inviting a group of young men on a retreat to go into a strip club? Unthinkable, yet it had just happened. I tried to dismiss the whole situation, giving him the benefit of the doubt that he just meant to make a joke, albeit in very bad taste.

The next day, back at the monastery, the priests offered Mass for all of us. But during Communion when I went up to receive, the priest broke off a chunk of what looked like leavened, regular bread, and handed it to me saying, "the Body of Christ."

I did my best to not let any crumbs fall, since this was the consecrated Host, but I went back to the pew confused. They had used leavened bread instead of unleavened bread for the Eucharist. I had heard that the Eastern Orthodox Christians did this as well, so while I believed it be a valid Mass still (and it was), my understanding was that Roman Rite Catholic Masses were to use unleavened bread. Why did these Carmelites decide to do differently? I never got an answer to that question

On the retreat, I had the most in common with one young man in particular. His name was John. He and I talked quite a bit because we were both similarly committed to discovering God's call for our life, which we both thought could be the priesthood.

As the weekend was drawing to a close, John took me aside and said in a very sober voice, "Devin, these are not the Apostles."

I understood what he was saying right away. And though I was a bit taken aback by how bluntly he expressed it, I had to agree. This was not how the Apostles lived nor was it how I envisioned living as a priest.

A Surprise at My Home Parish

I went back home and called up my parish priest. He knew that I was thinking about the priesthood, so he invited me to spend an afternoon with him. He really loved music and worked constantly on the pipe organ in the church, so he took me out to the workshop beside the rectory and showed me all the different pipes he was working on.

Our conversation turned to the priesthood, and he said to me offhandedly, "Devin, you don't need to worry about celibacy, because I know that the Church is soon going to allow married priests."

I felt bewildered. I had learned that symbolically the priest is married to the Church, and this is why priests as a rule are not married. Only in exceptional circumstances, like when an already married Protestant pastor became Catholic, could he potentially be given a dispensation and be ordained a priest.

I had worked hard to not be disturbed by the odd and contradictory opinions from the priests and religious that I had met. But I wondered: were there no Catholic clergy who adhered to what the Church taught? Why were so many spouting ideas that contradicted 2,000 years of Church Tradition?

In meeting these confused priests and religious, the thought ran through my head, "What if God *needs* me to become a priest, so that I can be a faithful one who will offset these others?" The fear that God "had it in for me" and would call me to be the one lone priest among a sea of unfaithful ones crept into my heart.

One thing I knew was true: I should keep praying the Rosary. I did so, even as I continued reading about different religious communities and tried picturing myself as a priest, ignoring the heterodox stuff that I had heard from actual priests.

Providentially, I heard from an old college friend, the same one who had given me St. Louis de Montfort's *The Secret of the Rosary* and started me on this devotion. He had entered religious life with a new Franciscan Order that was closely following the original life of St. Francis.

As I learned about this Order, who devoutly prayed the Rosary everyday during Eucharistic Adoration, I saw that even amidst the confusion and error that I had encountered, God had raised up new, healthy shoots from the solid roots of the Church's tree.

I learned all that I could about this Franciscan Order and asked our Lady in the Rosary if I should join it, too. It was then, in the depths of prayer, that I received the grace of understanding that although this Order was beautiful and holy, my particular call was to be married.

I knew that the priesthood was not my calling, but through my study I had gained a deep appreciation for the nobility of the priesthood and the great honor it was to stand in the person of Christ and offer the sacraments to the faithful.

I also realized that God does not "have it in for me" but that He loves me truly and wants me to be happy and fulfilled. He would not call me to be something that would be abhorrent and repulsive to my very self.

I did not have to live in servile fear of God; rather, He was my loving Father who wanted me to have a future of hope.

How to Mix in This Ingredient

The Rosary! This devotion is indeed an ingredient of the saints. It was given by the greatest saint, our Lady, to another saint, St. Dominic, for the purpose of making *us* saints.

My recommendation is that you pray the Rosary regularly.

I will admit to you that I had many people give me that same advice, and for years I resisted it. Perhaps for a week or a month I would pray the Rosary regularly, then I would slack off from the practice and quit praying it.

I encourage you to start by learning how to pray the Rosary if you do not already know and then begin with one decade per day.

The Rosary is broken up into four sets of mysteries, and each set is broken up into five decades. For instance, the Joyful Mysteries are the first set, and the five decades that make up this set are the Annunciation, the Visitation, the Nativity, the Presentation, and the Finding of the Child Jesus in the Temple.

Each decade consists of praying one Our Father, ten Hail Marys (hence, "a decade"), and then a Glory Be and the Fatima prayer.

Praying one Rosary consists of praying all five decades of one of the sets of mysteries, and that takes around twenty minutes. But praying only one decade can be done in five minutes. You simply choose a single mystery, for instance one of the Sorrowful mysteries like "Jesus Carries His Cross" and then pray the decade of prayers while meditating on that mystery.

Start with one decade per day and build up to a full Rosary.

Once you have prayed the Rosary several times, you can discover and explore more aspects to it. Not only are there four sets of mysteries (Joyful, Sorrowful, Luminous, and Glorious), but also traditionally a particular set is prayed on certain days of the week, varying also by which liturgical season the Church is currently in (e.g. Lent, Advent, Easter, etc.).

Finally, while you can start with rosary made of cheap plastic, I recommend buying a higher quality one made of stone, wood, or metal, and you should ask a priest to bless it.

We now have four ingredients in your secret recipe of the saints. Remember, I am revealing these ingredients to you as I discovered them in my own life. As you read this book, you can and should begin incorporating the ingredients into your own life.

But, near the end of the book, I will share with you the ideal way to "mix all the ingredients together for the recipe." Some of the most important ingredients I only found later in my life and wished I had discovered them sooner. But you will benefit from learning them now and being able to put them into practice.

Let's find more ingredients!

The Recipe of the Saints

The Bible
Eucharistic Adoration
Catechism of the Catholic Church
The Rosary

CHAPTER 5

Slavery to Sin

"Blessed are the pure in heart, for they shall see God."
—Matthew 5:8

I had now been Catholic for two years and had decided that my vocation was to marriage, not the priesthood.

While continuing to grow as a Catholic, I struggled with one habitual sin that had plagued me for years, through Protestantism, and into Catholicism.

That sin was lust, addiction to pornography.

I wanted to be free from this vice for many reasons. As a Protestant, I had read in the Bible where Jesus said that everyone who lusts after a woman has committed adultery with her in his heart. My heart told me that lust was wrong, the Bible agreed, and the Catholic Church authoritatively condemned it as a deadly sin.

Also, I worried that I would bring this addiction into my future marriage. I cringed when I imagined the idea of my wife discovering that I had this vice and the betrayal that she would feel. If she found out during our courtship or engagement, she may not even want to marry me.

Finally, Jesus said that everyone who sins is a slave to sin, and I wondered if I was really a son of God when I habitually committed these sins?

The Theology of the Body Discovered

As a new Catholic, I prayed the Rosary, read the Bible and Catechism, and had a weekly Holy Hour of Adoration, yet I still fell to the sin of lust regularly.

I felt shame going into the confessional again and again—often to the same priest—who no doubt recognized my voice.

I kept trying and trying to overcome lust, but it seemed to be two steps forward and one step back. I might go a week or two without falling to the temptation, but then the power of it would overcome me. I would feel a compulsion that I could not resist.

This caused me great internal consternation, because in the Bible St. Paul says that when we are tempted, God will not abandon us, but instead He will give us a way out of the temptation so that we can escape (1 Corinthians 10:13).

I believed that that was true, so it must mean that God was giving me a way out. Still, I could not find this way out. That made me question the quality of my faith. Did I really believe what I said I did?

It was during this time that I discovered something that would transform my understanding of sexuality: the Theology of the Body.

The Theology of the Body was a set of teachings given by Pope St. John Paul II during a series of Wednesday audiences in Rome over the course of four years from the late 70s to early 80s.

In the Theology of the Body the Pope described what happened to humanity when Adam and Eve committed the first sin. For the first time, a person could look upon another person as an object to be lusted after for selfish pleasure rather than as a person to be loved, created for their own sake in God's image.

I wanted to learn more, so I bought the full book of the Theology of the Body, which had been translated from the original Wednesday audiences of the Pope. It was deep, dense, and often beyond my comprehension. But I was gleaning many truths from it, and intellectually I was understanding the battle between love and lust that went on in my soul.

Pope John Paul II died shortly after I discovered his Theology of the Body, and now he has been canonized as a saint. I was so grateful to God that He had led me to this ingredient in the secret recipe of the saints, because through it I began to grow stronger in purity.

The Angelic Doctor Instructs

Along with the Theology of the Body, I came across the teachings of another saint: St. Thomas Aquinas, known as the "Angelic Doctor" due to his heavenly insights into God's wisdom.

One of the truths that St. Thomas Aquinas taught was that practicing one virtue would strengthen you in the practice of other virtues. A virtue, you'll recall, is a good habit that always is in the middle between two vices, which are bad habits.

For instance, the virtue of courage helps one confront fears and dangers, avoiding the vice of cowardice on the one side and foolish rashness on the other.

The virtue of generosity leads one to give in a wise way, the extreme vices on either side of it being stinginess that refuses to give anyone anything and wastefulness that imprudently gives things away to anyone.

Growing in one virtue will help you grow in the others.

Because the virtue of chastity is self-mastery applied to our sexuality, I began to practice self-mastery in other areas of my life: eating, waking up early in the morning, exercising, and praying and spiritual reading. In learning how to master myself in these other areas, I grew in strength in mastering myself in the area of purity.

Even with these great helps, I kept falling to temptation. It was a horrible cycle of being tempted, resisting for a while, failing, going to Confession, resolving never to fall to that temptation again, going for some time and keeping my resolution, before once again sinning and going to Confession.

What if I couldn't defeat this sin? What if I was going to be enslaved by lust forever?

The Breakthrough

The Theology of the Body had taught me that love was self-gift, and I knew that lust was simply taking pleasure by using another person as an object (even virtually through pornography). Even though I was still falling to temptation, this new understanding was equipping my mind and reshaping my heart, and I started to detest the sin of lust.

One day, after falling to the same temptation yet again, instead of having a good feeling from it, I felt completely empty and disgusted. God took the façade of lust completely away, and I realized what a lie from the devil that it was. I longed for the real love of marriage.

I refused to give up, and for the first time I went one entire month without lusting. Then another. Two months in a row was a record for me, and I realized that if I could do two months, I could do two years.

I saw that God could conquer any sin, even a deeply rooted one.

I woke one morning and my heart was filled with joy at the wonderful hope God had given me of a future free from compulsive sin. I could breathe more deeply. The dark cloud that overshadowed me due to lust was dissolving.

Now I could look at women and see them as beautiful, made in God's image, a tiny manifestation of His own uncreated, majestic beauty, and I did not have to lust after them. I rejoiced that now I would not bring lust into my marriage.

Still, I did not declare victory over lust, because every day I faced temptation, and I would not commit the sin of presumption by thinking I was above ever falling to the sin again.

But through this vigilance and God's grace, I had conquered it. The feeling of freedom that I had was magnificent. No longer did I have to live in the shame of remorse after falling for the umpteenth time to the same sin.

How to Mix in This Ingredient

With Pope John Paul II's Theology of the Body and St. Thomas Aquinas's explanation of virtues, you have an intimidating set of writings and materials to dig through. Here are my recommendations for unpacking these valuable but dense works.

Theology of the Body

If you are a big reader and also fairly adept theologically, you can go right to the source and read *Man and Woman He Created Them: A Theology of the Body*, translated by Michael Waldstein from Pope St. John Paul II's original words.

For most Catholics reading that book is too daunting. So my general recommendation is to pick up Christopher West's book, *Theology of the Body for Beginners*, which is a readable introduction to the content that will give you the understanding you need.

Our culture is so distorted and confused about all topics related to sexuality. It is frightening to see the rapid descent we are making into every manner of immorality and perversion.

The Theology of the Body is a key ingredient in fighting this diabolical poison. In it, you will discover how sin marred the original innocence in which God created Adam and Eve, causing the human heart to now be a battleground between love and lust, with Christ's redemption and grace offering us the capability of choosing to love rather than use other people.

It is truly good—and liberating—news.

St. Thomas Aquinas

If you thought the Theology of the Body was a thick book, wait until you see one by Aquinas!

St. Thomas Aquinas is the greatest scholar in the Church's history. His intellectual penetration into the truths of the Faith are unequaled. He developed an incredible harmony between faith and reason, most notably in his work, the *Summa Theologica* (also sometimes just called "the Summa").

If you have a background in philosophy or theology, go ahead and buy a copy of the Summa and read it. For everyone else (which is 99.9% of Catholics, myself included), you should take another approach to the work of Aquinas.

I recommend you start with Dr. Edward Feser's book, *Aquinas (A Beginner's Guide)*, which is a readable introduction to Aquinas's philosophy and theology.

One final note: tackling the Bible, Catechism, Theology of the Body, and Aquinas all in one go is a no-go. It's too much. Pace yourself. Start with one and then as you have the time and mental bandwidth, add another in.

Aquinas's work isn't going anywhere, nor are the others. They'll be waiting for you when the time is right. The journey that you have started on as a Catholic, perhaps a journey you started by reading this book, is one that will last your lifetime. No one becomes a saint overnight. Each day take one step forward with incorporating these ingredients, and you will progress toward sanctity. And don't worry, near the end of the book I will be giving you the full recipe and the how-to steps for mixing each ingredient in.

First Look, Lionheart Catholic

Overcoming lust is incredibly difficult, especially if that vice has had a long time to take root.

The first online course that I ever made was geared toward helping Catholic men conquer this sin and grow strong in purity. That course still exists, and Catholic men continue to sign up for it.

Men who sign up for the course get personal help from me on their struggle, including accountability partner matching based on age and state in life (married, single, children / no children).

Making this course showed me the benefit of having a community of Catholics all working toward the same mission (in this case growing in purity). It paved the way for a more expansive vision that became Lionheart Catholic.[3]

3   https://lionheartcatholic.com

Lionheart Catholic is a community of Catholics who are seeking to band together to incorporate the secret recipe of the saints into their own lives so that they can become saints, renew the Church, and transform the world.

I will share more with you on Lionheart Catholic in the next chapters, but first I want you to understand all the ingredients so that you have the tools you need to become a saint.

The Recipe of the Saints

The Bible
Eucharistic Adoration
Catechism of the Catholic Church
The Rosary
The Theology of the Body
Aquinas's Virtue Principles

CHAPTER 6

Courtship to Marriage

"Husbands, love your wives, as Christ loved the church
and gave himself up for her."
—Ephesians 5:25

I had now been Catholic for four years and had conquered the habitual sin of lust.

I longed to find the woman that God had chosen for me and be married so that we could begin our life and become saints together.

First Dates as a Catholic

I met some young Catholic women in my local area, but I had not worked up the courage to ask any of them on dates.

I feared rejection, common enough in such situations for any guy but exacerbated by my history of anxieties. One day I decided that I was never going to find my future wife if I didn't talk to any young women, so I prayed for the grace to talk with a cute girl that I had been seeing at Mass.

I approached her and said hello, and the first thing she said was, "I was wondering when you would finally introduce yourself to me." That made me feel pretty good, and we went and ate lunch together and got to know one another.

After a few dates, I learned that she enjoyed the Austin bar scene downtown (perhaps too much), and then she told me that she'd learned the most about the Catholic Faith from reading a book by Dan Brown called *The Da Vinci Code*. I almost fell out of my chair. This book was full of blasphemy and outright errors about the Catholic Church, and this young woman was reading it like the Gospels. I realized that she was not the right woman for me.

The Luck of the Irish

As a Catholic, I wanted to serve those in need in tangible ways, and I had learned about the Saint Vincent De Paul Society, a group that visited people in need in the community, giving them aid by helping them pay their utility bills, getting them connected with services in the area, or buying them food and clothing.

I had started volunteering each week with the Saint Vincent De Paul Society, and a dear old Irish couple who also volunteered introduced me to a lovely young woman who went to our parish.

We went on several dates, and I was hopeful that our relationship would turn into a serious courtship, but one evening over a milkshake she let me know that she didn't think I was a good fit for her. I was disappointed, because she was a solid Catholic who was also kind and beautiful.

"Back to the drawing board," I thought with weariness.

My First Catholic Mentor

I was blessed during this time to meet a man, Kenneth, who became a mentor figure to me.

His family sat in the pew in front of me at daily Mass. He had four children at the time, all of whom were respectful during Mass, and I could tell that he and his wife were devout.

Eventually we started talking after Mass, and we became friends. Kenneth was fifteen years older than I and so had a great deal more experience as a Catholic man than I did. He was also a husband and father, which I desired to be.

Kenneth explained to me that I needed to establish myself, who I was, where I was going in life, and then invite a young Catholic woman to join together with me on the journey.

I realized that a woman wanted a guy who knew what he was about and where he was going in life and that I did not often exude such confidence. I resolved to seek ways to grow stronger as a Catholic man.

My First Catholic Courtship

Months passed, and I turned 25 years old. I was working as a software developer in Austin, Texas and living with my old buddy, Gerardo, who had led me into the Church. I spent my time working, volunteering as a Big Brother to a boy who had no father, and playing soccer in the city's men's league.

But I longed to fulfill my vocation to be married. By God's grace, I started a Catholic courtship with a young woman and began to hope that here at last was my future wife. She was the younger sister of a friend of mine, a guy with whom I had grown up playing soccer.

Her name was Lindsey, and she had recently graduated from college with her degree in art. She was a talented painter, and while we did not know each other well growing up, since she was "just the younger sister" of my buddy, now she was a lovely young woman, and we began to get to know each other.

She shared my enthusiasm for Pope John Paul II's Theology of the Body, and she was devoted to the Holy Family of Jesus, Mary, and Joseph. We began to spend a lot of time together, and soon we were officially in a courtship.

Things went well for a while, but then Lindsey and I found ourselves getting into disagreements. To me, they were simply misunderstandings, but for her they cut more deeply. Nonetheless, we worked through them, and I began to have strong hope that she was going to be my future wife.

Over the next year, our relationship flourished. We spent almost all our free time together, and I went on trips that she took with her family to the beach. I couldn't imagine another woman who would be as good a match for me as was Lindsey.

Since her father was not in the picture, I decided that I would ask her mother for permission to propose to Lindsey, so one day when her mother and I were sitting alone on their back patio, I expressed my feelings for her daughter.

Her mother had reservations due to the fact that Lindsey had been in a serious relationship prior to ours, one which had ended painfully not long before she and I had met. Lindsey's mother was not sure that her daughter was ready to be engaged, but that if I was determined, she would give her consent to propose, and then Lindsey could decide.

A Proposal Gone Awry

I was determined to propose, and I began looking for a ring. I now know that I made a bad mistake here of thinking that, not only should the proposal itself be a surprise, but also the very fact that I planned to propose at all, I wanted to be a surprise. I should have discussed my intention to propose with Lindsey well in advance so that she knew a proposal could be coming.

As the day of my proposal drew nearer, an unfortunate situation happened where Lindsey and her mother were together, and Lindsey could tell that her mother was acting strangely and holding something back. Lindsey demanded that her mother tell her what was going on, and her mother explained that I had asked for permission to propose.

That news must have come at a bad time for Lindsey, because it shook her up greatly. She felt scared and not ready, but at the same time she did not want things to end with us. She shared with me her confusion and distress, and I sought to explain to her that I loved her and hoped that we could be married.

It was not to be. A few days later, Lindsey, with a heavy heart, broke off our courtship. I felt crushed. I had put so many hopes into our relationship and the desire to be married to her. Those dreams were now over, and all the time that I invested in our relationship went down the drain.

I turned to God in my grave disappointment: "Lord, couldn't you have just made this work? She was a faithful Catholic woman, and I know that she would have been a great wife."

I wondered if the problem was with me. Was I not worthy to be someone's husband? I had now been working for several years, living as a single man, and every single dating relationship, introduction, and even this courtship had gone south. I was moving into my late 20s and started to fear that perhaps I would never find my future wife.

A New Ingredient for the Recipe

During the next two years, I had no relationships. To make matters worse, my roommate Gerardo met a great young woman, and he started spending most of his time with her (they later married). I often came home to an empty apartment. Holidays were the worst, with all my friends gone to visit their families. Here, the loneliness really took hold.

I had lots of time to read though, and I felt that God was going to show me the way through this lonely time by reading good books. One day while reading a book on the saints, I came across the practice of fasting. I learned that it was a spiritual discipline that all the saints practiced.

I was particularly inspired by the life of St. John of Matha, who lived in the twelfth century at a time when Muslims were enslaving many Catholics. St. John was faithful from an early age, and after he was ordained a priest, God gave him a specific mission to ransom Catholics enslaved by the Moors.

Before St. John took on this difficult calling, he fasted and prayed for a long time. Always obedient, he then journeyed to Rome and asked the Pope for confirmation of this mission. The Pope also fasted and prayed, shortly thereafter giving St. John his wholehearted approval.

St. John thus began the Order of the Holy Trinity. He and his Order fasted everyday, and they begged for ransom money. They then took those alms and went to the Muslim countries where they ransomed Catholic slaves back to freedom.

I was inspired by St. John of Matha, but the fact was that I really hated fasting. On compulsory fast days like Ash Wednesday and Good Friday, I took advantage of all the fine print, eating two small meals that didn't equal one meal, in addition to one full meal.

And when I did fast, I felt terrible: hungry and sometimes nauseated with a headache.

But St. John had done it so heroically that I believed I could do something much smaller. So I began to offer a regular fast from food for my future wife, once per month on the first Friday, and I committed to our Lord that I would continue the fast until He brought her and me together.

While this new fast was a difficult thing for me to do, I figured that the difficulty meant that our Lord would value it all the more, as it showed that I was serious in wanting to meet my future wife.

Going Online

One of my friends told me that there were two Catholic singles websites that he was thinking of joining. I acted only mildly interested, but when I went home I started exploring them.

This was still in the early days of the internet, before smartphones, and even before secular online dating sites were common. Finding your spouse online was unheard of at the time. Nonetheless, I figured I should place bets on all possible options and not rule out any means that God might use to bring me together with my future wife, so I joined both sites. I had all my bases covered.

I corresponded with various young women, but nothing ever amounted to a courtship.

Every month or so, I would correspond with a young woman on the sites, but none progressed far, and I began to lose hope that this was a route that our Lord would lead me to my wife through. I considered closing my accounts down and ending the whole idea.

Another Secret Ingredient Found

Still feeling lonely, I kept on reading books. God has already introduced me to fasting through reading, and I wondered if He had more in store for me.

In one of my books, I came across something called a novena, a nine-day prayer wherein you ask a saint to intercede for you for some intention. I started researching them and found out that the St. Joseph novena could be prayed for the purpose of finding your future spouse.

I found the specific set of novena prayers in a book I had on St. Joseph, and I began praying, asking of St. Joseph the gift of being brought together with my future wife. Less than a week later, while I was still in the middle of the novena, I saw a new young woman's profile pop-up on one of the Catholic single sites. Her name was Catherine.

Catherine's profile jumped out at me, because she seemed intelligent, devout, and also funny. She gave a little litany of things that made her go "yuck" that included credit card debt and fast food. (Personally, I was also against credit card debt, but not so much against fast food!)

I messaged her through the site and was delighted when she responded.

We corresponded for a week, after which I abruptly received a message from her saying that she was going to be talking with another young man and was no longer interested in corresponding with me.

"Well, that's that," I thought. This experience was not uncommon in the world of online correspondence, where it's so easy to start or stop communicating with someone, so I didn't let it bother me too much.

But to my surprise, a week later, I received a message on the other Catholic site that I was on. It was from the same Catherine, and apparently she had joined that other site too. She didn't say anything about how she had brushed me off and cut off our correspondence. Only very briefly she said "Oh how funny to see you here on this site as well!"

At this point, I wasn't playing any games, so I candidly asked her, "When we corresponded last, you ended it. Do you want to correspond or not?"

She later revealed to me that she appreciated how straightforward I had been with her. She explained that the other young man was not a good match for her and that I came back into her mind shortly thereafter. I was happy to resume our correspondence, as we clearly had a lot in common together. She had discovered her Catholic faith in college at Notre Dame and was quite devout.

Dodging Bullets

Through our correspondence, I learned that Catherine was the director of a pro-life organization in Kentucky, a fact which impressed me, because since becoming Catholic, I had realized how important the plight of unborn children was and had become involved in the pro-life movement in Texas.

I asked Catherine if we could talk on the phone, and we set the first phone date. The day came with excitement, but that phone call was incredibly awkward. We only sort of knew each other from email correspondence, and we just didn't seem to click. I wasn't too worried about it, because I figured this type of thing happens, so we set another date for our second phone call.

That phone call felt stilted as well. We were just not on the same wavelength, and it felt like a very forced way to communicate with each other when we had never met in person.

Little did I know that after we got off the phone, Catherine was ready to break off our communication, deciding that I wasn't a good fit for her. I don't blame her: based on conversations I was thinking the same thing. But I was willing to give the benefit of the doubt and wait a bit longer.

We had our third phone date set, and Catherine was ready to deliver the bad news to me then, I later found out. But one evening, a few days before our scheduled phone call, I decided to call Catherine spontaneously on the way home from work.

It caught her by surprise, and we had a fun, easy conversation that flowed smoothly. We laughed together. I made jokes and let my guard down. It disarmed her, and we had a really good conversation.

So far we had dodged two bullets, first when she had initially brushed me off and then when our phone calls didn't go well, and she had planned to end our relationship.

But a third bullet was coming.

We decided to meet in person, and since it was Christmas time she was at her family's house in New Mexico. I got on a plane and flew to meet her in her hometown.

We met outside an Italian restaurant in the little downtown area. We both felt awkward, because even though we'd been corresponding for a few months and talked on the phone several times, it's something different when you're face-to-face for the first time.

We spent the afternoon together, and then I went back to my hotel. Catherine had gone back to her home, and she talked with her mother about me. She told her mother that she did not think that I was the right one for her. We had had another awkward time and did not seem to have chemistry. Her mother, though, had seen something in me and counseled her daughter to give me one last chance.

One Last Roll of the Dice

Back at the hotel, I prayed the Rosary and asked our Lord for His wisdom in what I should do. In answer to prayer, I got the idea to just relax and have a fun time on our next date.

The following afternoon, I went over to Catherine's house to take her to a lovely Italian restaurant. Much to Catherine's dismay--and my embarrassment now--I showed up for the date dressed in old jeans and a free T-shirt that I had gotten from a 5 kilometer race I had run many years ago, along with beat-up sneakers.

I have to admit that I did not have a good eye for style or fashion, and I put very little effort into my wardrobe. I figured that what mattered was what was on the inside. While that is true enough, now I shudder when I think of how I must have looked to my future wife: tennis shoes, poorly cut jeans, free t-shirt.

Even so, Catherine had committed to her mother to give me a chance, and on our drive to the restaurant I put on a special CD that I had made with songs I really liked. By God's grace, one of those songs by a Christian band was one of Catherine's favorites, and we found ourselves both singing the song together in the car. Few things bring people closer than singing together, without embarrassment, trusting one another and enjoying the time.

The chemistry sparked that night, and we had a great conversation. I learned her history, and she learned mine. I realized that she was just the woman for me.

Later on, she revealed to me that in Adoration our Lord had said to her that I was going to be her husband. This was well before I had even flown out to meet her in person, and she didn't know how it would come true given that we had had so many awkward interactions.

Engagement and Marriage

I proposed, and Catherine said yes.

We were engaged, so we collected her belongings and drove from her family's home in New Mexico to Austin where I lived. Friends of mine graciously said that she could stay at their house while we were engaged, so we set the wedding date and prepared to be married.

After six months of engagement, we got married in her hometown. The wedding was a Nuptial Mass that started with the Holy Rosary and included many traditional flourishes that are rarely included in wedding Masses nowadays. We held our reception at the local vineyard and winery, and God sent a short rain shower just before it began, cooling off the New Mexican evening and making for a festive atmosphere.

In my time as a single man, and even leading up to meeting Catherine, I feared that I was not good enough or worthy to be a husband. But God in his great love showed me through my courtship, engagement, and marriage that by His grace, He did make me good enough. I was worthy to be Catherine's husband.

We are now in our second decade of marriage, and, as you will see in subsequent chapters, while it has not been without great trials, I wouldn't trade it for the world.

How to Mix in This Ingredient

Fasting

Fasting has been a key spiritual practice in the Catholic Church since the beginning. Only in the past 60 years or so, has the practice of fasting has been greatly downplayed. Fasting has potent spiritual benefits, allowing us to recognize our total dependence on God: we don't live on bread alone, but on every word that comes from the mouth of the Father (Matthew 4:4).

While I discovered fasting and its spiritual benefits before getting married, it was not for another decade that I would realize its many physical benefits. These benefits are now being recognized in the medical world as well. Intermittent fasting has caught on as a very healthy practice that people can use to improve everything from their cholesterol, to their blood pressure, and for weight loss.

When I found out that my blood glucose was in the warning zone and that I was going to get Type 2 Diabetes in the next year unless I made big changes, I learned about intermittent fasting. In reading more about it, many of the myths that I had associated with fasting were dispelled.

Intermittent fasting has many variations to it, but the one that I practiced the most was eating only one meal per day (typically dinner). Some days I would eat two meals but concentrate them in a single four-hour block of time. Eating in such a way gives your body long periods of time where your insulin is low, which reduces any resistance to insulin that your body may have built up from frequent eating.

So I began doing intermittent fasting for my physical health, and it reversed my slide toward Type 2 Diabetes. But I also make it doubly effective by offering my fast each day for some spiritual intention: for a person I know who is in need, or a virtue that I needed to grow in, or for my family.

I now see that the physical benefits of fasting are one more of these providential designs that God has given us, knowing that we are each a substantial union of both body and soul. By learning how to intermittently fast, I am no longer afraid of fasting like I used to be.

So I recommend that you start to fast[4] and read about inter-mittent fasting. Best practices have been developed that make fasting more understandable and bearable, even enjoyable at times.

Novenas

Novenas have become one of my favorite ways to pray.

Over the centuries, novenas have developed in quite a wide variety of sizes and shapes. You have the traditional nine-day long novenas, typically asking for the prayers of a particular saint, for a particular intention, but you also have novenas of varying lengths, like the 30-day Novena to St. Joseph, the 25-day St. Andrew Christmas Novena, and the 54-day Rosary Novena.

The primary benefit of novenas is that you are dedicating yourself to prayer for a particular intention, and we know that God answers prayer. A secondary benefit, however, is that in praying a novena, you learn more about the saint whose prayers you're requesting. After finishing a novena, I feel like I've gotten to know that saint better and that we have a special kinship.

If you have not prayed a novena before, I recommend finding one for a saint that you're already devoted to. Lots of novenas exist online, or you can also use the Pray Catholic Novena app[5] that I have developed.

I also recommend joining with others in a novena. This is especially powerful if you have friends and family with whom you wish to pray, perhaps for a mutual loved one who is in need. You don't have to physically pray the novena together

---

4   Consult a doctor on this as I am not one. Some people should not fast, and others should do so only under medical supervision.

5   https://pray.app.link/get-the-app

but rather can both be praying the same novena at the same time, knowing that your friend or family member is praying with you for the same intention.

You can't go wrong with praying novenas. It is a beautiful devotion, and one that I hope you also will discover the wonderful blessings from.

The Recipe of the Saints

The Bible
Eucharistic Adoration
Catechism of the Catholic Church
The Rosary
The Theology of the Body
Aquinas's Virtue Principles
Fasting
Novenas

CHAPTER 7

A Faith Worth Defending

"Always be prepared to make a defense to any one who
calls you to account for the hope that is in you, yet do it
with gentleness and reverence."
—1 Peter 3:15

Six years out of college, and I was happily married.
I had made lots of friends at my tech job, including some
Protestants. They challenged my Catholic beliefs, and our
lunch times developed into an informal Catholic-Protestant
debate club.

Tongue-Tied

I was eager to defend my faith, and I dreamed of the day that
my friends would see the truth of Catholicism, as I once had.

To make the stakes even higher, my mother had surprised
me by returning to Christianity after decades of agnosticism.
She was going to a Protestant church and came to me with lots
of questions and arguments. I found myself defending Catholicism on multiple fronts.

Often times in these discussions with my friends and my mother, I would feel tongue-tied, not knowing the right answer. I would often say that I needed to go do some research and that I would respond the next time we met with what I had discovered.

One would think that I would know my Catholic Faith inside and out, having been a convert from Protestantism. That's what I had thought, too. But while I had learned enough to convince *myself* to become Catholic, others were not convinced by the same arguments. Or their concerns about the Catholic Faith were different than the ones I'd had.

I knew the Bible pretty well and the competing Catholic and Protestant interpretations on many important verses, but I needed a greater degree of understanding to tackle my friends' arguments.

Fear of a Killer Argument

But here was the problem: whenever Protestants made arguments against Catholicism, I felt defensive. Deep down I feared that I had made a wrong decision in becoming Catholic. I dreaded coming up against a killer argument that Protestants might have against Catholicism and discovering that, even though I loved my faith and was deeply convinced by it, I had done something foolish in becoming Catholic.

This hidden uncertainty made questions about my faith feel like personal attacks, and I would lash back with whatever came into my mind at the moment. One friend of mine, David, was the best software developer at my company with a brilliant, analytical mind. He attended a Baptist church.

He and I were acquainted with each other, but we became friends when he found out that I had played soccer. He was looking for someone to coach his son's soccer team. I agreed to be the coach, which led to David and I spending more time together.

When he learned that I was Catholic, he told me that he had never met a Catholic who actually seemed to believe in Jesus Christ. I was the first one whose faith seemed to matter. He wondered why I was Catholic, and why I had not remained a Baptist like he was.

We entered into a long series of conversations, some which lasted many hours. We went back and forth about Catholic and Protestant issues. Whenever I made a really good argument against Protestantism, he would go and research and come back with a response the next time, and vice-versa.

But we eventually came to a standstill. He was not convinced by the arguments I gave, and I was not convinced by his arguments. I wasn't sure what could break the standoff, so for the time being we tabled it.

Quaking in My Boots

I had another friend at work, a soft-spoken man named George. He went to a Quaker Church, and I learned that Quakers were Protestants who met in silent assemblies with no pastor and that when a member of the assembly felt "moved by the Holy Spirit," that person would then go up to the front and speak to the rest of the congregation about what God had just told them.

I learned that there are multiple strains of Quakerism, and some of them more like mainstream Protestant churches, but the version that my friend, George, practiced was this silent, unprogrammed kind of Quakerism.

When I began conversing with George, I did not know much about the history of the Quakers, so I did my own research. I learned about their founder and how he had been dismayed when he saw so many people who purported to be Christians, all baptized, yet acting in immoral ways.

The Quaker founder concluded that water baptism must not do anything and must not be vital for salvation. He started a new denomination, the Quakers, because of this belief.

Because Quaker and Catholic teachings on baptism differed so substantially, my conversations with George centered heavily around the sacraments. I argued that baptismal regeneration was true. Catholic doctrine states that, when we are baptized, we receive the Holy Spirit and are cleansed from our sins. We receive God's sanctifying grace in our souls, making us friends with God.

As we got deeper into our conversation, George began to get frustrated with me. One time I told him something about Catholicism that was inaccurate—I was still learning and didn't always get everything right—and he decided that I was not being completely honest with him. So for the time being, he closed off further discussion. I was disappointed and tried to explain that I unintentionally made an error, but he was unmoved.

At the same time, I was having an ongoing conversation with my mother. She had objections to Catholicism which were different from either George's or David's. She protested Catholic practices like not eating meat on Fridays, which she said seemed legalistic and not in line with the Gospel of Jesus.

Even after I explained that not eating meat on Friday was just a discipline and not an unchangeable doctrine, she remained hung up on it. I realized that I needed to delve deeper into the concerns that she had rather than just dismissing them. I began to do that, but she remained unconvinced with my answers even then.

I felt flummoxed. I had hit a wall in all my discussions. I couldn't shake the feeling that there was some weakness or deficiency in me that was failing to convince my friends and family that Catholicism was true.

The Great Saint Apologists

While I had read several good, modern apologetics books, I wondered if any of the saints had dealt with these Protestant arguments. Soon after, I learned about St. Francis de Sales and St. Edmund Campion. Both men were notable apologists, defenders of the Catholic Faith.

When I read St. Francis de Sales's apologetics writings, I was stunned. He had already responded to every important issue with Protestantism, and his answers were clearer and more compelling than mine. This discovery was a great relief to me, because it meant that I didn't have to deduce by myself how to respond to Protestantism's challenges. Instead, I simply had to learn and then repeat what men much smarter than I, and holier, had already figured out long ago and simplified for me.

I learned that, four hundred years ago, St. Francis de Sales went to Switzerland, where the Calvinist Protestants were strong, and after years of evangelizing these Calvinists, he had made zero converts. I could relate.

Instead of giving up, however, he persevered and invented the religious tract, kind of like a pamphlet, which he slid under people's doors. As he walked around the cities, towns, and countryside, he prayed constantly, beseeching God to move every heart back to the true Faith. Our Lord blessed his labors: 70,000 Calvinists renounced Protestantism and returned to the Catholic Church.

Another Catholic hero was Englishman St. Edmund Campion. As a young man, he was Queen Elizabeth's most promising and faithful Protestant scholar. But as young Edmund learned about the historical faith of England, he realized that it was not Anglican Protestant in origin, but rather Roman Catholic.

He left the Queen's service, sailed to France to train with the Jesuits and was ordained to the priesthood. He then secretly returned to the English shores to minister to his countrymen.

During this era in England, being a priest meant death by painful execution. Even sheltering a priest was dangerous. The Holy Mass was forbidden, and faithful Catholics in England made secret compartments to hide priests when the English authorities came.

St. Edmund was eventually betrayed and captured, and the Queen's men tortured him. Between the periods of torture, they dragged him into a courtroom and made him stand before a set of Protestant scholars to engage in debate. He had been physically and emotionally exhausted by the horrible tortures inflicted upon him.

All the Protestant scholars had ample preparation and stacks of books in front of them, but St. Edmund was given no books, no paper or pen, and no help from anyone. Even so, as the people in the audience watched the debate, St. Edmund refuted the Protestant scholars again and again, on point after point of Christianity. The debate was eventually ended, and St. Edmund was brutally martyred at Tyburn Tree in London.

I found entire books by these saints online, and I read them carefully over the next several months, writing down important points that I knew would help me with my mother and friends. Before my next conversations with them, I read over my notes and rehearsed in my own mind how to put their wisdom into my own words.

One noble quality that I observed in these saints was how gracious they were in their debates, even against unfair odds, torture, and hatred. These men responded with kindness and grace, and this more than anything stunned the audiences who watched them, leading many of them to convert to Catholicism later. I wanted to be like them, not just to have the right responses, but to respond in a way that was gracious.

Putting the Lessons Into Practice

I realized that, in being afraid of a killer argument from Protestantism, I had not acted with grace, but rather with knee-jerk defensiveness. I resolved that, when I continued my conversations with George, David, and my mother, I would act differently and imitate the saints.

When we resumed our conversations, I tried to listen patiently. I began to see the deeper issues underlying the surface concerns that they were raising. Instead of reacting, I dug down until I truly understood what they were really asking, and then I went and looked for the best answer.

Months went by, and George initiated new conversations with me about Catholicism. I noticed though that his demeanor had changed. Before, he was guarded and suspicious of me, but now he had an openness toward me. He also brought up new subjects and seemed to have resolved our old topics of disagreement internally. For my part, I resisted getting frustrated or reacting in fear when he spoke of things that I thought I had explained already.

In the online world, I frequented a website where Catholics and Protestants debated each other in a blog format. Around this time I saw that George was commenting with questions to the Catholics on that forum. It helped me better understand where he was coming from so I had more context about what he was thinking.

To my amazement, a few months later George told me that he and his wife had decided to become Catholic. He asked my wife and I to be his eldest daughter's godparents, which we happily agreed to.

When it rains, it pours, and after even more months of intense conversations, my mother surprised me when she said that she had decided to enter RCIA. She went through two years of RCIA before she felt ready to enter the Catholic Church, but she completed the classes, and also entered full communion with the Church.

David, however, did not become Catholic. But something quite surprising, and even miraculous, happened. He revealed to me that he had had a vasectomy years prior after the birth of his second child when he and his wife felt that they just couldn't handle another child.

Now, he told me that he and his wife had a change of heart. They wanted to have another child. I said, "Oh wonderful, so you are going to get your vasectomy reversed?"

But he shook his head and said he had no intention of reversing the vasectomy. Instead, he confidently told me that he expected God to act miraculously on his prayer request for a child, and he said that, if God wanted them to have a child, God would conceive one in spite of his vasectomy.

I told him that this was a way of testing God, since David had not done all that he could as a human being to fix the issue. He got defensive and told me that I did not believe as strongly as he did in miracles.

I left it at that, but a year later he came up to me and said that he had gotten the vasectomy reversed and that they were expecting their third child! That child was born, and a few years later a daughter followed, giving them four children.

I felt blessed and grateful to our Lord to have been a small part of that miracle of new life. When I asked him what had changed his mind on the vasectomy reversal, he said that, some months after he and I last spoke on the subject, God had directly told him to get the procedure done. I was so thrilled that I didn't care how he had gotten the message, through me or directly from God.

Through each of these conversations, and my own study, I had finally become convinced that nothing could disprove Catholicism, that there was no killer argument that could destroy the Catholic Faith. I felt free and light-hearted.

As a Protestant I had sung a song that said, "I'm happy to be in the truth," and now, as a Catholic firm in my faith, I knew that that lyric was really true. Christ had built His Church and guided it into all truth, just as He promised. While I may fail to always follow this truth, I was rooted deeply in it, secure and safe.

My faith was finally my own. The saints had showed me the way, because with their superior intellect and study of the Faith, none of the arguments that Protestants brought up held water.

I gave thanks to our Lord for confirming me in the truth of Catholicism.

How to Mix in This Ingredient

Defending Your Faith

Learning how to defend your faith, and doing so with grace, will give you greater confidence whenever you enter into discussions with non-Catholics.

These two secrets of the saints—apologetics and grace under fire—will help you to lead your friends and family to greater virtue and maybe even into the Catholic Church. I have been blessed to experience such conversions a handful of times, and I want you to experience it as well.

In my own life, I usually have to defend my faith against Protestants. Because of that, I have focused most of my efforts in understanding my faith on topics that Protestants are most interested in.

If you also want to defend your faith against Protestants, you could go right to the source and read from St. Francis de Sales or St. Edmund Campion. However, I recommend a more readable, modern apologetics work. In fact, I wrote two such books!

My first book is called *The Protestant's Dilemma*. It breaks arguments down into bite-sized chunks explaining why Catholicism is true and why Protestantism simply does not work. Thousands of Catholics have read it and grown strong in their understanding of the Faith.

My second book is called *Navigating the Tiber*, and it both teaches the arguments you need to know to defend your faith and also equips you, step-by-step, to lead your Protestant friends into the Catholic Church.

Reading these two books is a good introduction into apologetics. You may also want to learn more about how to defend your faith against other kinds of non-Catholics (atheists, Muslims, etc.) and you can continue your journey of learning in those directions.

With some friends, you can almost always have a friendly, mutually beneficial conversation. Sometimes, however, the person you're talking to is aggressive, or combative. In these cases, you need a healthy dose of grace to practice kindness and prudence even when you're under fire, just like the great saint apologists of this chapter showed.

It's easier said than done, and you may get into a situation that is beyond your virtue. If so, and you just don't see how the conversation is going to be fruitful for either of you, it is okay to simply tell the person that you don't think that you both can discuss this type of topic for the time being.

I've had that happen many times, only to realize later that my friend and I found we were able to finally discuss these issues again. Take the long-term view: focus on your friendships, and know that people see how you are living your life, which will be one of the greatest witnesses you can have to them. They will then be wanting to talk with you to understand what is it about you and your beliefs that leads you to live in such a way.

No matter what kind of conversation you are having, you need to pray for your friend throughout it. Offer a decade of the Rosary for them, or a novena, or even a fast. Only by God's grace can they see the truth that you have, and prayer is the door to that grace.

Stump the Apologist, Lionheart Style

Defending your Catholic faith is not easy.

The second online course that I ever made was specifically to help fellow Catholics defend their faith against challenges from Protestants.

I've loved interacting with the members of that course. They ask me questions and tell me about theological challenges they are facing, and I equip them with the principles they need to know to answer these challenges.

I also did webinars, which are kind of like live video chats, with the members of this group. We got to interact together and "crowd-sourced" answers to the challenges members were getting.

I found this content and format so beneficial that I rolled it into the Lionheart Catholic community that I mentioned earlier in this book. We do regular webinars on a range of topics, including learning apologetics and defending your faith, where we all get to discuss what we are encountering and how to best respond.

I'll share more about Lionheart Catholic in subsequent chapters.

The Recipe of the Saints

The Bible
Eucharistic Adoration
Catechism of the Catholic Church
The Rosary
The Theology of the Body
Aquinas's Virtue Principles
Fasting
Novenas
Apologetics
Graciousness when under fire

Chapter 8

Infertility and Miscarriage

"Take courage; the time is near for God to heal you;
take courage."

—Tobit 5:10

W hen Catherine and I married, we assumed that we'd be blessed with a large family. It rained on our wedding day, and we joked that it was a divine sign of fertility. We hoped to be blessed with ten children and to join the ranks of big Catholic families who drove large vans and filled up an entire pew.

The first month after our honeymoon, Catherine took a pregnancy test. It was negative. So was the test a month later. We suffered our first miscarriage during our fourth month of marriage, the baby too little to even register positive on a pregnancy test. We named him Rafael.

In the sixth month of our marriage, Catherine was hit with a wave of nausea. This time the pregnancy test was positive.

Fleeting Joy

I was overjoyed, and amazed at the reality that I was a father. We soon had our first ultrasound, and we were able to hear our baby's heartbeat.

Several weeks later, however, Catherine started feeling fewer pregnancy signs. We went to the doctor, and the doctor told us that our baby had stopped growing. He should have been 10 weeks old in size, but he looked only eight weeks old, and he had no heartbeat.

Catherine and I were devastated. Very soon after the fateful doctor visit, we visited her family in New Mexico, and while we were there, Catherine started bleeding, slowly at first, but then she began to hemorrhage.

We realized that she needed to get to the hospital. But as she stood up to walk to the car, she went deathly pale and collapsed. She had no pulse and was not breathing.

I was there with her but was panicked and did not know what to do. All I could do was repeat the Hail Mary again and again. Catherine's mother was there and screamed at her that she could not die. Her mother was a retired nurse and began CPR. I turned to her father and in a shaky voice asked him to call 911.

Catherine later told us that she felt herself leave her body and during this time was looking at us from above. She regained consciousness as the paramedics came and took her in the ambulance, rushing her to the hospital. She delivered our deceased son, whom we named John Thomas. She had lost so much blood that she had to receive several blood transfusions.

A Saint Familiar With Trials

I had lost my second son to miscarriage and had almost lost my wife. Deeply shaken, I felt powerless to protect my wife and my child from what had happened to them. Why did God allow this?

In the following months, Catherine physically recovered, but emotionally we felt bereft and abandoned. During her recovery, looking for comfort, I discovered a treasure trove of Italian movies that depicted the lives of various saints, and one I watched with fascination was St. Rita of Cascia.

Rita was born in the 1300s near Cascia in Umbria, Italy. She wished to enter religious life from an early age, but her parents arranged her marriage at the young age of twelve–a common practice at the time–to Paolo Mancini. Though Paolo was wealthy, he was quick to anger and viceful. Already at a young age Rita was facing serious trials.

Rita bore Paolo two sons, but Paolo treated her harshly. He was physically and emotionally abusive, unfaithful, and entangled in an ongoing feud between rival factions in the area.

Instead of responding with anger or unfaithfulness herself, Rita responded to these trials with heroic endurance, longsuffering patience, and radical trust in God. Through her prayers and witness, her husband Paolo eventually repented of his evil life and embarked on changing himself. As part of his personal transformation, he refused to participate any longer in the feud, but in spite of this, he was ambushed and killed by a rival.

Rita publicly forgave her husband's murderers and sought to end any revenge attacks from the Mancini family. But Bernardo, Paolo's brother, instigated her two sons to join the feud and avenge their father. Rita's sons went to live with Bernardo and began to imitate their father's pre-conversion life of vice.

Fearing that her sons would follow their father and die a violent death, Rita beseeched God to prevent their taking revenge. A short time later, her sons died of dysentery, an unexpected answer to Rita's prayers that they would not die in mortal sin but an awful loss for her as a mother.

Rita was now freed to enter the Augustinian convent in Cascia, but her application was denied, because some of the nuns there were members of the family that had killed her husband. Undeterred, Rita stormed Heaven and enlisted the saints to obtain the grace for her to be admitted to the religious life.

She worked to make peace between the feuding families in Cascia, and in return, at 36 years of age, she was granted entrance to the convent. St. Rita trusted through all the trials of her life, even the most horrible ones.

I shared what I was learning with Catherine, and we decided to emulate her in this radical trust. Little did we realize that we would have the opportunity to put this into practice once again.

New Hope

The months that followed came with no positive pregnancy tests. Those months turned into years in which we didn't conceive, and we began to fear that something was wrong. We went to see the doctor, but he only gave us conjecture about what might be going wrong. He told us that because of how long it had taken us to conceive, we either had low fertility or infertility and offered to prescribe medication for us.

Through her pro-life work, Catherine had learned about Natural Family Planning (NFP), so she started charting and checking her signs, in hopes that that we would be able to conceive. After several months of charting, she delivered the happy news to me that she was pregnant.

Catherine had conceived, and we were ecstatic. Catherine quickly found an NFP-respecting OB/GYN, and began taking progesterone to help ensure that we would not lose our baby. Everything looked healthy in the ultrasounds, and as the months passed, we began to feel great hope that we would have a healthy baby.

During Christmas, she went into labor. I had never felt love such love for my wife as I did that night. She gave birth to our son at 3 o'clock in the morning. We named him Edmund, after St. Edmund Campion, and after Edmund Pevensie from C.S. Lewis's *Chronicles of Narnia* series.

Everything looked good. Catherine held Edmund and tried to nurse. She was bleeding, but the nurse said such bleeding was normal, and would lead to the placenta being delivered next. I didn't know what was considered normal bleeding, but after awhile Catherine started looking very pale causing immediate flashbacks to when we lost John Thomas, sending off alarm bells in my head.

Our inexperienced nurse was undecided about what she should do, so I asked her to go get the doctor. She halfway nodded, wavered, then left the hospital room, while Catherine continued to bleed.

A few minutes later the OB/GYN doctor came back into the room, went to Catherine without saying anything, did a rapid examination, and immediately yelled for her to be taken to emergency surgery.

Catherine, now alarmingly pale, handed me Edmund, whom I held close to my chest. It was about five o'clock in the morning. Our hospital room was cold. I was tired from being up with Catherine through the night, and I felt alone and isolated. I didn't know the first thing about what my baby son needed, or how soon he would need it.

I figured that he would get hungry, but I didn't know how to feed him. All the nurses had left with Catherine, so it was just me and my baby in the room, dark, cold. My mind was racing with fears: what was wrong with my wife? Would she be okay? Panic started to well up, and I forced it back down.

I wanted to go to my wife and be with her, but I had a newborn baby to protect. I was torn between my duty to my wife and my duty to my newborn child. I couldn't help them both at the same time.

I turned to God, asking Him to be with my wife and to give me wisdom with my newborn son. I thought of St. Rita. I thought of how she trusted God through every trial with her family. I didn't want to experience the death of a spouse like she did, but she was the model I would follow if God so chose to take Catherine. I sat holding my crying son. He must be hungry, I thought, or in pain. The panic started building again as I felt helpless about how to calm him down. No one came in to update me on how my wife was doing. I was in the dark in every way.

I got up and started rocking Edmund back and forth. I sang a little song, something from the pop music charts that just happened to be in my mind. Mercifully, his crying started to lessen and then he fell asleep. I laid him down in the hospital bassinet. Exhausted, I fell asleep, almost immediately.

I awoke a few hours later and learned from a nurse that Catherine had lost a lot of blood; her placenta would not detach from her uterus which had led to her hemorrhaging in an attempt to deliver the placenta. Through the surgery, the doctor had successfully removed the placenta. She was weak, but my wife was going to be okay!

Once again my wife Catherine had been in jeopardy, and once again I had been powerless to protect her. But God had brought her through safely. The realization hit me: I am not going to be able to protect my family from all evils and dangers in this world. Their lives are in God's hands, first and foremost, and our Lord was asking me to trust Him.

It was hard to trust God, because these things that happened were so scary, so outside my control, and so seemingly random. But I believed in faith that nothing was random, that everything that occurred was within God's providence, and so I need not fear that something would happen that He had not already foreseen and allowed to be.

After several days of recovery in the hospital, Catherine and I went home with Edmund, tired but grateful. Our Lord had not abandoned us. He brought us through, alive and together as a family. St. Rita had shown us the way, and we had trusted Him through a scary time.

Sooner than we would expect, we would again need to practice this virtue of trusting God through trials.

How to Mix in This Ingredient

You will have plenty of opportunities to practice the art of learning how to trust God during trials because, unfortunately, no life is without trials. The difficulty comes from the fact that when you are facing a trial, it is the moment when it is hardest to put your trust in our Lord.

During such times, I find making an act of faith, hope, and love helpful. These are traditional prayers they have been prayed over the centuries by countless Catholics, including the saints.

For instance, Pope Clement XI said these short prayers, which I memorized and encourage you to pray as well:

"O my God, I believe in Thee; do Thou strengthen my faith.

All my hopes are in Thee; do Thou secure them.

I love Thee with my whole heart; teach me to love Thee daily more and more."

The wonderful thing is, when we feel most helpless, but turn to our Lord during difficulties, our loving Father pours out even more graces upon us, for we are demonstrating to Him our faith, that even though we cannot see Him with our eyes, we believe that He sees us, loves us, and will act.

Trials do not always end in the way that we hope they will. Sometimes they result in the very thing that we most feared would happen. It is then that we have to turn to God and pray for the grace to accept what His will was on the matter.

I have found that it takes many years after the trial before I'm able to look back with perspective and see that there was anything good that occurred through it. Perhaps I can see that through the trial I grew as a person, grew in virtue, or learned an important lesson that I may not otherwise have learned.

Other times, I'm not able to see the good, and so I have to trust that our Lord did allow it for a purpose even if I don't know what it was.

Where are we now in our journey? We've now discovered over ten ingredients in the secrets of the saints. We are halfway to the full recipe. Imagine how much you will grow if you put these into practice, how close to God you will get, by His grace? With His help you can do it.

The Recipe of the Saints

The Bible
Eucharistic Adoration
Catechism of the Catholic Church
The Rosary
The Theology of the Body
Aquinas's Virtue Principles
Fasting
Novenas
Apologetics
Graciousness when under fire
Trust through trials

CHAPTER 9

A Princess Is Born

"Jesus offered up prayers and supplications, with loud cries
and tears, to him who was able to save him from death, and
he was heard for his godly fear. Although he was a Son, he
learned obedience through what he suffered."

—Hebrews 5:7-9

Our son Edmund was now a toddler, and Catherine and I
were thriving in our marriage.

Still, we continued to struggle with fertility, having another
baby miscarry, whom we named Jacinta.

Catherine and I still longed to have a big family and were
open to the children that God wanted us to have, but so far we
had not been blessed with many children.

Friends of ours asked us when we were going to have more
children, perhaps thinking that we were deliberately choosing not
to have them. Nothing could have been further from the truth,
and Catherine suffered emotionally with this for some time.

Finding an Ingredient in Suffering

As I continued reading more about the saints, I noticed another common hallmark: joy in spite of suffering.

I read story after story of saints who suffered tremendously, yet united their sufferings with those of Jesus on the Cross as a prayer for others.

My favorite saint, St. Therese of Lisieux, echoed this common refrain when she said that "sufferings gladly borne for others convert more people than sermons."

I wanted to put this into practice, so each suffering I faced, even small daily ones, I offered to God as a prayer for others. It felt strange at first, and took faith to believe that it made a difference, but I kept offering my sufferings, and each time it got easier.

Catherine had a great love for Pope St. John Paul II who at this time had only recently passed away. In his Apostolic Letter *Salvifici Doloris*, he wrote that:

"The Redeemer suffered in place of man and for man. Every man has his own share in the Redemption. Each one is also called to share in that suffering through which the Redemption was accomplished. He is called to share in that suffering through which all human suffering has also been redeemed. In bringing about the Redemption through suffering, Christ has also raised human suffering to the level of the Redemption. Thus each man, in his suffering, can also become a sharer in the redemptive suffering of Christ."

Inspired by this strong witness, Catherine and I resolved to imitate the saints in this regard as well, and offer our sufferings of infertility and miscarriage to Christ as a prayer for all those babies whose mothers did not want them, who were in danger of being aborted.

One morning, I woke up and went about making breakfast and getting ready while Catherine was still in bed. While I finished cooking the eggs, she came up behind me and said, "You should go and check in the bathroom. There's something you'll find there."

Amused, I went into the bathroom and noticed an object on the counter that looked like a pen. Upon closer inspection, I saw it was a pregnancy test; my excitement grew as I noted the positive indicator. We had conceived again!

New Life

Because of all the problems in our past, I never took it for granted that we would conceive another child. Though I was deeply moved and happy, I knew that with the multiple children we had lost to miscarriage, there was no guarantee that this child would survive to birth. I put a guard around my heart.

We had moved to a new city, and there was no Natural Family Planning OB/GYN in the entire metro area. As we researched, we found one about an hour west of the city in a small town. We started going to see her for appointments.

This doctor was fantastic, and she asked Catherine many questions about Edmund's birth, as well as about her miscarriage of John Thomas, when she hemorrhaged.

After an ultrasound, the doctor called us into the room and said, "I'm seeing something here with the placenta and your uterus that is concerning to me. There is a condition called placenta accreta, where the placenta fuses with the uterus, and it can make it hard for the placenta to detach and be delivered after birth. I'm going to be monitoring this, but you should be prepared for the possibility that you may have this condition."

As the months went on, Catherine and I read up on this condition and discovered there were three degrees of it, the most mild being placenta accreta, and the most severe being placenta percreta where the placenta grew completely through the uterus.

When we went to visit the OB at around seven months into the pregnancy, she told us that Catherine did not have not placenta accreta, but instead the worst kind, placenta percreta. She explained that this was a very serious condition and only one hospital in the state was equipped to handle it.

The Stakes Get Higher

We knew we were facing suffering again, but this time we did not let it beat us down to discouragement or despair. Instead, we united our sufferings to Christ's sufferings on the Cross, accepting that He had chosen to give us this cross to bear which we could offer as a prayer for others.

We did not just wish to be Christ's friends in His glory but also in His trials and sufferings. In this way, we tried to emulate the saints who meditated on all that Christ subjected Himself to on their behalf. Calling His sufferings to mind, they refused to complain, knowing that those who wished to reign with Him must suffer with Him. We strove to do the same.

Catherine and I went to visit the new doctors in the hospital where she would deliver the baby, but quickly became alarmed: they did not seem to have handled such a situation before. In fact they were discussing the situation as if it was an interesting "experiment," the outcome of which they could neither confidently predict nor guarantee. They asked if they could have medical residents watch in the delivery room, as if my wife's risky delivery would be no more than an educational experience for student-doctors.

Catherine and I went home and discussed our options. We decided that though the baby was due in just over a month, we were going to drive back to our original home city in a neighboring state, to our original doctor, stay with my mother, and give birth there where the hospital and doctors seemed more competent.

We packed up and made the interstate drive. We met with our old OB, who confirmed that Catherine's was a very serious condition that would require a C-section. The doctor's tone intensified as she also informed us of our worst fear: that in all likelihood, Catherine would have to undergo a hysterectomy, in order to prevent Catherine's death. We were now facing surgery, possible complications from her condition, and the likely loss of our ability to have any more children. My mind spun with the fear of what could happen.

The day of the surgery came. Catherine was scared but also resolute. She told me that she was offering her sufferings to Christ's and had accepted whatever His will was with her life. I tried putting on a brave face so that she would not see the anxiety gnawing at my insides. What if God's will was that she die?

The doctors were prepared for Catherine to lose a lot of blood. They inserted some sort of valves into her leg arteries that they could expand if needed to stop her from bleeding to death. The enormity of what could happen pressed down on my mind.

I was ushered into the delivery room with Catherine on the gurney. The doctors went to work, and I held Catherine's hand. I started getting choked up but shook the tears away. I had to be ready for anything. The doctors delivered Josephine via C-section. They gave Josephine to me, let Catherine give her a kiss, and then they rushed me out of the operating room with Josephine. Now was the dangerous time for Catherine, and they had to go to work.

I left the room with my baby daughter and prayed that Catherine would be okay.

I protectively held Josephine close to my body as a nurse took me to have Josephine weighed and measured. I caressed her little face. She was crying a little but then stopped.

As with the birth of Edmund, I waited with my newborn baby as Catherine underwent surgery. A calm came over me, and I silently began invoking the prayers of the saints, one-by-one. "St. Catherine of Siena, pray for us. St. Therese of Lisieux, pray for us. Our Lady, pray for us. St. Joseph, pray for us. St. Michael, pray for us." I beseeched our Lord to protect my wife's life and keep her with us. Josephine needed her. Edmund needed her. *I* needed her.

As the doctor held Josephine to weigh her and take her vitals and measurements, Josephine began to cry. But I started speaking to her in a soft voice, and she immediately pricked up her ears and calmed down. (While she was in utero, I had often spoken to her close to Catherine's belly so she would get used to my voice.)

It dawned on me that we almost certainly would never have another baby. I offered to our Lord the suffering of the permanent loss of our fertility. We had hoped to have so many children, but that dream was over now. I felt conflicted, because here before me was my beautiful, tiny daughter. She already was bringing me such joy. I couldn't wait for Catherine to hold her, too. But for so long we had dreamed of a big family, bursting with love and holy chaos. Now, we would be a small family. I couldn't yet accept it.

Catherine emerged from surgery, successfully, without the loss of a lot of blood. She was wheeled into the hospital room, and she called for Josephine to be placed in her arms. I gently handed our daughter to Catherine. Over the next three days in the hospital, as Catherine began recovering from surgery, we shared the great joy that we felt at the birth of our daughter but also mourned the loss of our fertility. It was a suffering that we could only begrudgingly offer to God, a suffering we never thought we would have to endure, nor one that we wanted. All the more reason, I believed, that God would use this suffering for good.

In the months that followed, as we reared our newborn and spoke of what had happened with Josephine's birth, we came to accept, through many tears, that God's vision for our family was very different from what we had hoped. Other Catholics thought that we were contracepting and had chosen to have only two children. Multiple times people said to us, "Oh, now you have a boy and a girl, the perfect family! You're all done."

We just smiled weakly at them. It was not worth trying to explain how very differently we viewed things. Through the suffering both of Catherine's condition during pregnancy and then with the loss of our fertility, we grew closer to our Lord through suffering. Jesus was a man familiar with suffering, and He was giving us the privilege of being like Him in this regard. If we suffered with Him, He had promised, we would also rise with Him.

How to Mix in This Ingredient

Read the life of any saint, and you will encounter them suffering in some way. It is a constant that is found in every saint's story, and that includes your own.

Whether it was St. Therese of Lisieux, and her desire to be a missionary in foreign lands, which was never satisfied except through prayer, or St. Maximilian Kolbe, who gave his life for a fellow prisoner during World War II, each of the saints faced sufferings. But what was remarkable was *how* they endured that suffering.

Consider the lives of the martyrs, for instance the Japanese martyrs, who each of them faced torture and horrific pain but did so with joy. This reaction of joy is not natural. It rubs against our human grain. It is only possible to do with God's grace.

So when you are suffering, whether it be physical pain or emotional, tell our Lord you are uniting your suffering to His on the Cross; you can offer a prayer intention to go along with that suffering. Mysteriously, God invites us to join Him in the suffering He endured, and doing so joins us to His redeeming mission.

St. Paul wrote about this in Colossians 1:24 when he said, "Now I rejoice in my sufferings for your sake, and in my flesh I complete what is lacking in Christ's afflictions for the sake of his body, that is, the Church."

Christ's sufferings are not lacking in any way, rather St. Paul, like us, had been given a share in those sufferings, to bring the gospel and Christ's love to people. Sometimes, when we are suffering, and we unite our sufferings to our Lord's, we do not feel any tangible comfort or consolation. It is instead a pure act of faith, and thus is pleasing to our Lord.

The Recipe of the Saints

The Bible
Eucharistic Adoration
Catechism of the Catholic Church
The Rosary
The Theology of the Body
Aquinas's Virtue Principles
Fasting
Novenas
Apologetics
Graciousness when under fire
Trust through trials
Uniting sufferings to Christ's

CHAPTER 10

Green Acres

"Count it all joy, my brethren, when you meet various
trials, for you know that the testing of your faith produces
steadfastness. And let steadfastness have its full effect, that
you may be perfect and complete, lacking in nothing."
—James 1:2-4

Early on in our marriage, Catherine and I found out that we
both had a fascination with beekeeping.

And so before our children were born, we had actually gotten bees, bee suits, and all the equipment and had been keeping
bees for several years.

But we were also intrigued by the idea of having a farm.
We liked the idea of raising our own food: it would have fewer
pesticides and chemicals in it and, therefore, be healthier. We
also wanted to have the security and independence of having
our own land and being able to grow our own food.

Along with these ideas of eating in a healthy way, we wanted to preserve our children from what we saw as a very toxic
culture. Being out in the country would afford us a measure of
insulation from the big city.

We also observed how our country had been degrading morally at a frightening pace, and we feared that if our country continued in the same direction--and there were no signs indicating that the degradation was slowing--that eventually we would have a societal implosion.

Land Ho!

We looked for land in the area and found a nice property with over ten acres of land about a half hour from the city where we lived.

Once we moved out to the farm, we quickly ramped up our operations with animals, which included chickens, guinea fowl, rabbits, and cows. I would rather not have had cows, but maintaining our agricultural land tax exemption (an "ag" exemption), which gave us a big tax break on the land each year, required that we had at least seven cows.

There was a learning curve with every aspect of the farm, from how to buy a tractor and then operate it, to how to stop the wild animals from eating our guinea fowl (spoiler alert: we failed at that and all our guinea fowl were eaten).

We had hoped that we would have good neighbors who would be friendly and helpful, but one neighbor we never saw, and the other one was not so much interested in being helpful but rather in pointing out things we were doing wrong.

"Helping" Our Neighbor

Despite the seemingly endless difficulties, after a few months in our place, it started to feel like home. My software job allowed me to work from home a few days each week, and we were finding a routine. The amount of farm work needing to be done each day continued increasing, but I felt sure that it would eventually climax, and then I would start to get ahead of it.

One Saturday, our neighbor, Ms. Susan, came up to the fence and asked if I would help her with a donkey that had caught its foot in its halter. Wanting to be a good neighbor, I agreed and walked over to her place. She led me to her barn and quickly stepped into one of the empty pens, closing and latching the gate closed behind her. I stood sort of stupidly in the middle of the path through the barn, but it wasn't clear to me what she wanted me to do. She was fiddling with some things when the first animals came galloping into the barn.

Two horses, then two donkeys, then five goats, then three of her middle-sized pigs, all came clamoring in for what I began to realize was feeding time. The barn was fairly large but soon seven more horses, seven more donkeys, two huge pigs, and several other animals stampeded in, and I was surrounded by the hungry beasts.

The four-hundred pound pigs in particular alarmed me. I knew enough to know that a pig can have you for lunch without too much trouble. I climbed up to stand on top of the nearest stall gate, and said, "Ms. Susan, am I safe here?"

She looked up at where I was, holding onto the rafter atop the gate, and said, "If *you* feel safer where you are, then you should stay there." It was not very comforting, a sort of Zen answer implying the animals could sense my fear and that walking among them in such a state would be practically inviting my demise. The blame would be mine, presumably, because I failed to exude an aura of confidence.

I made the command decision to stay where I was. But apparently I had chosen the wrong stall. Because the two biggest pigs, Daisy and Pork Chop—I kid you not those were their names—began bellowing like they were being slaughtered. I didn't know if they just wanted their food or were angry at me for standing on top of their stall. Still bellowing, both lifted up their huge bulk and slammed their fore hooves on the top of the gate that I was standing on, four feet off the ground.

I crowded against the post trying to avoid them. If they could get their hooves up that high, they could leap at me and knock me into the melee. Catherine would later tell me she and the children were outside near our fence, listening to the pig-shrieks, wondering if I was being gored to death.

Just when I thought the animals' bellowing could not get any louder, they heard Ms. Susan pouring their feed into the troughs. The pandemonium and noise redoubled, and the animals were shaking the stalls and gates, including the one I was on.

I was now really frightened. I looked for some way to escape, but there was none. Ms. Susan continued puttering about, showing little concern for any of the hullabaloo. She went through little secret doorways in between each stall, putting food out into them. Then she lifted up the latches and let the animals into their respective stalls.

As the animals poured in, I slid around the post and got onto the top of the next stall's gate, then jumped in, a safe distance from the still-bellowing pigs. I heard them hogging at the mash she gave them and breathed a sigh of relief.

I could see Ms. Susan entering a crowded stall in which nine donkeys milled about. The one we were after had its foreleg in the halter and had rubbed it raw. She was trying to catch it so we could free it.

I could only think of the stories I had read of donkeys biting people's arms and causing great bruising, or their famous kicks from their hind legs. I helped Ms. Susan as best I could, and at last she got the donkey and freed its leg.

Being someone who liked to chat, she tried to tell me about the time she had found all these donkeys roaming wild after a forest fire occurred in our area a few years prior. But I hastily made my excuses and bolted out of there as fast as I could walk without making it look too obvious.

One crisis averted. Clearly though, this neighbor was not going to be someone we would be good friends with.

As the months went by, we grew lonely. The small parish in the neighboring town was anemic, and there were almost no families who we could befriend. We petitioned our bishop, asking if we could invite several different religious Orders to the diocese, because there was land available for them to build a monastery, but our bishop turned down each request, citing fears that such a religious community would cannibalize donations that would otherwise go to the diocese.

And so we came upon unexpected consequences of being out on the farm: we were isolated from community and with regard to our faith.

Back Breaker

Nonetheless, we are able to handle all of the animals and the expenses, but just barely. That was, until one day when I had worked very strenuously on the farm, moving big hay bales around and clearing heavy brush over the fence. The next day I noticed my back was hurting. No big deal I thought. I took two Ibuprofen and went back to work at the computer.

A few hours later the pain had doubled, and ibuprofen was having no effect. I began to get worried, because severe waves of pain were coursing through my lower back. A few hours later, I was in so much pain that I had to lie down, ice pack on my back.

I hoped that the pain was temporary, but to my dismay, it was not. I didn't think the pain could get any worse, but the next day it did, so much so that I could not work, sit down, or even stand up for any length of time. I had really done a number on my back.

I got a friend to drive me to the chiropractor, who said I would probably be fine in a few weeks, then did an adjustment. I was not fine in a few weeks, and I was barely able to do my work.

I became very afraid that I had compromised my ability to provide for my family. What was I going to do? Not only did I have my regular computer work, but I also had cows and animals to take care of, and I could barely function.

After a month, the intense pain subsided a little, but if I did anything out of the ordinary, even lifted the lightest of weights, or did any farm work, the back pain would come back with a vengeance. Sitting at my desk was extremely difficult, so I got a sit-stand desk attachment, allowing me to alternate between sitting and standing. That made it just barely endurable.

Job Switcheroo

I became even more alarmed when it became clear that I needed to change software jobs. I found a position at a new company, but it was even farther away in the city, requiring an hour drive each way from our farm.

When we had moved out to the farm, I had sold my smooth driving commuter car for a big, old pickup truck, so each day I drove into my new job, and the truck would jar and bounce my back painfully.

I was trying to do a good job at my new work, to show them that I was competent, and I did not dare to let on that I was in severe back pain. But it was a startup company, and they demanded a lot.

I was given a computer with an operating system I had never used in order to program a new mobile app, a type of programming I had never done, and meanwhile my entire back was inflamed with pain.

To get through each day, I slathered on "Icy Hot" lotion over my neck and back. Problem was, the smell bothered my coworkers. So I could not use it as frequently as I wanted to. I was also taking aspirin or ibuprofen every four hours, just to keep the pain from exceeding my tolerance. I was going to the chiropractor and getting back massages whenever I could, doing all sorts of treatments, attempting to stave off surgery.

My mind raced with fears: what if I became incapacitated and couldn't work anymore? How could I provide for my family with such awful pain? How could I bond with my children when I couldn't even pick them up and hold them without causing intense physical suffering?

I finally broke down and went to the spine surgeon. He did an MRI and said I had two ruptured discs, with the fluid leaking out of them. The discs were becoming desiccated, dried out, and therefore offering no cushion between the vertebrae.

He said that before trying surgery, which he thought I would eventually have to have, we could do an injection in my back. I did that injection, but unfortunately during it, the injection needle pierced my spinal column, causing fluid to leak out. The doctor cursed when he realized he had done that, and they made me lie down immediately, because, he informed me, due to the pressure loss in the spinal canal, I was about to get a massive headache, and if I stood up, I would get dizzy and fall.

I did get that massive headache, but after a few hours the pain subsided, and I was able to go home. The spinal injection temporarily helped my back pain for about a month, but that was all.

A Saint Familiar With Suffering

During this time, I read the story of Saint Bernadette and Our Lady of Lourdes. Bernadette was a poor French girl who lived in the mid-1800s and to whom our Lady appeared many times. Bernadette was uneducated, simple, and devout. She and her family had many troubles, and after our Lady appeared to Bernadette, many people in the town persecuted her, accusing her of making up the whole story of seeing the Virgin Mary.

Our Lady showed Bernadette how much she was loved in Heaven, but also gave her to understand that she would suffer in this life. She told Bernadette: "I do not promise to make you happy in this life, but in the next." Bernadette would only find happiness in Heaven.

Bernadette desired to be a nun, but when she entered religious life, she was humiliated as the Mother Superior and Bishop spoke of how stupid and useless she was (right in front of her!). Because of her perceived uselessness, the bishop gave her a single assignment: simply to pray and be a nun.

At the convent, the nuns were told to be on guard against her and not give her special treatment simply because our Lady had appeared to her. St. Bernadette endured all of this humiliation with grace.

She had had cholera as a child, which had left her with severe asthma the rest of life. It also led to her developing tuberculosis in her lungs and bones, causing incredible pain. She succumbed to her illness and died at a young age.

113

Tail Between Our Legs

I thought about the fact that our Lord, speaking through Mary, told St. Bernadette that happiness in this life was not promised, but in the next life it is. I decided that I had to stop trying to force the farm to work and really think about what God was directing us to do.

Catherine and I sat down together to talk about the farm. I asked her if she liked it out in the country, and did she want to stay. At first, she was hesitant to be completely honest, because she thought that I wanted to stay on the farm no matter what. But I assured her that I wanted her frank and candid feelings.

In a rush, she told me how lonely and isolated she felt on the farm. She longed to be with other families, in a neighborhood, in a community. She missed the activities and civic events that were so easy to go to in the city. The farm also weighed on her mind, because it was never "done." There was always more work to do, more things to put in order, to fix, and with my back, I could never get to it all.

Relieved, I told her that I thought God was making it clear to both of us that we needed to move back to the city. So with my ability to provide for my family jeopardized, and the farm being too much, we had to give up our farm dream. We put the farm up for sale and sold all of our animals and equipment, only making back some of the money that we had spent. Still, it was enough to move back into the suburbs, tail between our legs.

Upon hearing the news, many people we knew couldn't resist saying, "we told you that you wouldn't be able to do it." Well, they were right. I wanted to preach back at them about how if you never take a risk and dare to push your limits, you will never achieve much, but I held my tongue.

All told, for three and a half years I suffered with back pain, doing everything I could to avoid surgery, but ultimately the ruptured discs between the vertebrae were gone, and I had a spinal fusion surgery for the three vertebrae. Thanks be to God, the surgery was successful, and I was able to work again without severe pain.

While it was not bad to have a dream of owning a farm, I realized from this experience that I can't make Heaven here on earth by my own power. Our Lord made that fact clear to me both through the failure to invite a religious Order to our area and through our failed experience farming. Instead, I needed to ask God how our family could work toward holiness even in the suburbs of a big city.

If our society went down in degradation, the best I could do was protect my family from it, and train my children to be prepared to face it, with virtue and love.

How to Mix in This Ingredient

Are you looking for happiness? I know that I am. God made us to be happy, happy with Him forever in the eternal life of Heaven.

This side of Heaven, however, is the problem. God never promised us happiness here, but that of course does not mean that we shouldn't seek happiness. It is our human nature to want to have comfort, peace, and friendship. If we can live in luxury, it is natural to want to do so.

That said, Jesus gave us supernatural reasons to *not* love luxury, when He said that it is harder for a camel to go through the eye of a needle than for a rich man to enter Heaven.

What we need is balance. Sure, I always try to avoid suffering and things that make me unhappy, but our Lord has brought things into my life, like hurting my back severely, that I was not able to avoid.

Compounding the physical pain and fear of not being able to provide for my family, is also the emotional stress of wanting to be pain-free and yet enduring pain everyday. I have found it helpful to remind myself that here on earth I'm not promised a happy life or an easy one, and this life is actually what's best for me in order to reach the far more important goal of eternal life.

Eternity is a long time, and our temporal life here on earth pales in comparison to what that eternal life will be, which we cannot even imagine. So when I face pain, unhappiness, and stress, I seek to call to mind what our Lady told St. Bernadette, that she cannot promise happiness in this life, but only in the one to come.

This reminder sets my expectations properly, because I have always been tempted to look forward to the future when, say, I would have enough money saved for retirement. "Then I'll be relaxed and happy," I've told myself.

But then I see examples of people I've known, friends of my parents, who did retire, and yet they were no happier than when they were working. One friend had just retired, and her lung collapsed due to COPD from a lifetime of smoking. Her retirement years will be spent permanently on oxygen support.

While that situation is a dramatic example, and that particular suffering is to a large degree self-inflicted, I'm sure you too have known stories of people who retired only to have a heart attack or stroke and pass away or be debilitated. Through it, our Lord shows us that there is something more important to focus on than bodily health.

We want to be storing up treasures in Heaven, where moth and rust do not decay and thieves do not break in and steal. For as our Lord said, where your heart is, there will your treasure be.

The Recipe of the Saints

The Bible
Eucharistic Adoration
Catechism of the Catholic Church
The Rosary
The Theology of the Body
Aquinas's Virtue Principles
Fasting
Novenas
Apologetics
Graciousness when under fire
Trust through trials
Uniting sufferings to Christ's
Happiness in the next life

CHAPTER 11

Sued!

"You have heard that it was said, 'You shall love your
neighbor and hate your enemy.' But I say to you, Love your
enemies and pray for those who persecute you, so that you
may be sons of your Father who is in heaven; for he makes
his sun rise on the evil and on the good, and sends rain on
the just and on the unjust."
—Matthew 5:43-45

We were now back in the suburbs, and I had a software job
at a consulting company.

But the experience with my back showed me that relying
on a corporation to pay the bills was an uncertain foundation.
Ideally, I would be able to own my own business that would
bring in income regardless of whether I was able to work all the
time or had a back problem that kept me from working.

I liked the idea of having this security and freedom from a
corporation, who could decide to not employ me any longer
for many reasons, but also I dreamed of being able to be home
with my family, work from home on my own terms, for my
own self, so that I could do all the things with my children that
I longed to do.

New Business Launched

I made the decision to quit my job at the consulting company, and along with two of my co-workers there, we started our own software consulting business.

As we started our new company, we needed to find clients. I had already found one client, so that brought in some income for us, but I and the other two founders were working full-time, and one client could not cover all our salaries. So two of us received no salary, and my family lived off savings while we sought to build the business.

After a few months passed, I began to feel anxious that I had made a poor decision about whom I partnered with, because of a disagreement that arose as we were drawing up our company's operating agreement. Specifically, I explained to my business partners that I did not want to do business with certain types of companies, including ones that published pornography, and they bristled at my explanation.

My business partners were atheists, and therefore had not the same moral objections I had. I explained to them my strong objections to doing business with certain industries, and that I would not compromise my beliefs.

Instead of saying, "Devin, we understand and respect your conscience," they said, "We outnumber you, and our company operates through majority agreement, so we can outvote you in such cases."

In the past, my wife had expressed to me her concerns about who I had chosen as my business partners. I had not listened to her, but now I began to fear she was right. She started asking for the prayers of St. Therese of Lisieux, that God would show me how I should proceed in this business. Those prayers would come into play in a remarkable way shortly.

For the next month, I continued to live off of savings, each day going into our business to try to find new clients. While we had a few leads, it took quite a bit of time to fill the pipeline and close deals.

My two business partners wanted us to have greater visibility in the area, so they wanted to do some types of marketing that were possibly going to provoke our former employer. We had all signed non-compete agreements with our former employer, but so long as we did not poke the bear, I felt all would be well.

I objected to us taking any action that would rouse the ire our old bosses, but the other founders outvoted me and went ahead and did what they wanted.

Legal Trouble

Less than a week later, we received a registered letter in the mail, a cease-and-desist letter sent by lawyers who had been retained by our old company.

They demanded that we cease our business operations immediately. My anxieties went through the roof, as here again was a new threat to my being able to provide for my family, as well as my dream of owning my own business, of having security.

Frantically, I entreated my business partners to begin acting with prudence, to placate our old employer and take down the materials that had provoked them. But both my business partners were roused, and, instead, wanted to fight our old company.

Rather than taking actions that could have de-escalated the conflict, they inflamed the situation even more, and the following week we received the official lawsuit from our old company against our new company and against us individually for violating our non-competes.

That lawsuit arrived on St. Therese's feast day. My wife and I looked at each other with a grim, foreboding look. Our Lord was showing us something through St. Therese's prayers, and it was up to us to listen.

But in the meantime, I had a legal fight on my hands. I had never been sued before, and the unknown elements of it caused me quite a fright. Could we go to jail? Could they sue us into bankruptcy? How do we navigate the complex legal system?

Instead of looking for new clients upon which to build our fledgling business, we spent almost all the days in legal preparation with our lawyers, trying to figure out how we could win the lawsuit.

I went home everyday emotionally wrecked. I was on the verge of panic attacks again, something that had not afflicted me for fifteen years. It was hard to get my mind to think of anything else but the lawsuit, and I began to research bankruptcy laws, trying to figure out what all they could take away from me and my family.

Legal Gray Area

Was I in the wrong in starting this new software consulting company? The answer to that question is not straightforward.

Before I had resigned from my former employer's company, I had spoken to the owners and told them that I was working on my own with specific clients. They made no objections to this work, since the clients that I was working with were too small to be of interest to them. That fact naturally led me to think that they had no problems with my consulting business.

But obviously they changed their minds later on and must have decided that we were a threat to them. It felt spiteful, as if they simply didn't want us to be successful. From my perspective, the world was plenty big enough for two software consulting companies to coexist without issue. My anxieties doubled as each day passed and the legal machinations became more involved.

A Saintly Way Forward

I needed to find some way to be at peace, even amidst this stress. By God's grace, I discovered that many saints wrote about the need for *detachment*. They resisted (or broke off) attachments to created things: to comfort, wealth, people, earthly security.

I had been reading a long poem by St. John of the Cross, and though his writings often went over my head, I understood this one part, where he said, "In order to possess everything, do not desire to possess anything."

By "possess everything" he meant possess God, who is everything. It was a paradox, a "true contradiction" because only by detaching from the world could I find peace in the world. The saints all practiced this holy detachment, and when their oppressors or the circumstances of life caused them to lose material things—friendships, wealth, titles, and honors—it did not disturb their peace.

As I struggled with the anger and fear at the people suing me, I found this powerful quote from St. Francis de Sales, who said: "Do everything quietly and in a calm spirit. Do not lose your inner peace for anything whatsoever, even if your whole world seems upset."

I realized that I was letting my former employer cause me angst and stress, and I was losing my inner peace everyday. I decided I did not want to give them that power over me. I asked myself, "What's the worst that could happen?" They take away all of our "stuff" and empty our bank accounts. We will still have each other as our family.

I started trying to discover what material things I was attached to and actively detached from them.

Even though both our legal arguments and our opponent's had some merit to them, I was tempted to feel resentment and even hatred for my former employer for putting me and my family through this. It felt like they were using the courts and their money as a weapon against me and my family.

I felt the desire to get them back, to strike fear into their hearts, to make them feel financially afraid like they were doing to my family. But it was a saint again who quelled this thought: a bishop named Fulgentius lived in the 400s and early 500s, during the time of the Arian heresy, which denied Christ's divinity.

Fulgentius was betrayed by an Arian priest, was scourged brutally, then had his hair and beard plucked out, and was left naked in the street, battered black and blue. It was said that even the local Arian bishop was aghast at how shamefully and viciously St. Fulgentius was treated, and told him to give him the Arian priest's name so the bishop could punish him.

St. Fulgentius said, "A Christian must not seek revenge in this world. God knows how to right his servants' wrongs. If I were to bring the punishment of man on that priest, I should lose my own reward with God."

St. Fulgentius lived Jesus' words to love our enemies, and pray for those who persecute us.

Would I defy the saint and our Lord's words by seeking revenge? No. While I was not yet ready to forgive my enemies, I decided to refuse to hate them, and instead I prayed for them.

Legal Games

In the lawsuit, we defeated one legal motion that our former employers tried to prosecute against us, which would have caused us to shutdown our business operations.

It was a short-lived victory though, because a few days later they simply added the motion back in on top of another motion, and because we had a different judge that day, the new judge granted the same motion that had been denied by the previous judge just a few days ago.

I realized that the legal system could be gamed, that lawyers can use lots of tricks in order to manipulate how the system works and that our lawyers were not as crafty as theirs. This new motion granted a temporary injunction against our business.

Instead of letting this defeat spiral me into a new cycle of panic, I detached myself from all of it, and I prayed for wisdom from our Lord. I was the CEO of our company, but this was not the ship that I wanted to go down in.

Our Lord showed me that I should step down as CEO, resign from the company, and go get a job so that I could pay the bills and lawyer fees, and if we lost the lawsuit, any damages.

I went into our office that morning, and I told my business partners I was resigning from the company, effective immediately. They were angry with me, accusing me of abandoning them by refusing to fight. I told them that the fight had caused me too much stress and that trying to start a business while being sued was simply too difficult.

I told them that I was sorry, but it was not going to work, and I got into the proverbial lifeboat and started paddling off to shore. Now that I had resigned as CEO of the business, I helped to broker a conversation with our former employer, and we worked to settle the lawsuit. We found a mutually agreed-upon settlement, where no money changed hands. The only ones who won were the lawyers.

I then found a job and started working immediately, so that I could avoid going into debt to pay all the legal bills.

I had dreamed of owning my own business, providing for my family without being at the whim of a big corporate employer, but that dream had ended again. Our Lord showed me that money won't buy me security, nor will my own business. Those things can be quickly snatched away by anyone deciding to bring a lawsuit against you.

In hopes of finding that security, I had rushed into a business partnership with guys who did not share my morals or values. Realizing now how foolish that was, I also realized that our Lord had brought wisdom to me from it, teaching me detachment. I had learned that even if I went bankrupt and lost everything materially, what counted was not sinning against God, and loving my family.

How to Mix in This Ingredient

Man, oh man, is it hard to practice detachment and love of your enemies.

These two ingredients, like suffering, are ones that you usually don't have to go looking for. They find you.

Detachment

The opportunity for detachment arises often, typically when we find ourselves deprived of something that we really want.

Maybe our house got foreclosed upon. Maybe a beloved friend moved to a different town. Maybe we lost our job and were faced with the double stress of having no income and losing the prestige and status we had in our own minds from the job we worked at.

We get attached to things of this world very easily. But the virtue of justice demands that we only give created things their due attention and concern. It is to God that we must look, who created all these things, and give Him our full heart and mind.

Loving Your Enemies

This ingredient, which of course Jesus commanded us to do, is a curious one. What I have noticed over and over again, within myself and even among other Catholics, is an unwillingness to recognize when someone is our enemy.

Back in the Old Testament, the enemy was obvious: that other tribe of people that was coming to wipe us out. Or, that jealous man is trying to kill me. There's your enemy alright, no problem.

But in our modern times, enemies are rarely so easy to identify. Instead, you may have an enemy at work, who has been criticizing you behind your back to other coworkers, stirring up people's perceptions against you, and only later you realize it when you discover you don't get a raise or are pigeon-holed in some way at your company.

You may discover an enemy in someone you thought was your friend, but who, it turns out, perhaps was incapable of being a true friend, of truly loving you. And you only find out years down the line that this person has been manipulating you or always trying to take from you while rarely or never giving back.

Are such people always enemies? No. Sometimes they are doing their best, and they are just very wounded, so their capacity to love is handicapped. Nonetheless, I find it helpful to identify when someone is an enemy, rather than seeking to explain their behavior away, because then Jesus' words apply, and I can put them into practice.

Jesus said to love your enemies and pray for those who persecute you. So right from the outset, you can pray for these people, for their conversion and salvation. You hope to see them in Heaven one day (and how awkward would it be if you met them in Heaven and realized that you had not prayed for them as you should have?).

Loving them is wanting what is best for them. That does not mean that you have to be their friend. It may mean that the best thing for them (and you) is to put distance between yourselves, or even break off whatever relationship you may have with them completely.

Deciding in each situation how to love them is something only God can show you in prayer. (A wise spiritual director helps as well though such a one can be hard to find nowadays.) The important thing is that you fight against your natural inclination to take an eye-for-an-eye, and instead do whatever you can to love them.

Most likely, their harmful actions are causing wounds and jeopardizing their own souls, causing offense to God, and this is the most important reason for your wanting them to stop their wrong actions. These ingredients are difficult to mix into your life, but they are essential for the recipe to turn out right.

The Recipe of the Saints

The Bible
Eucharistic Adoration
Catechism of the Catholic Church
The Rosary
The Theology of the Body
Aquinas's Virtue Principles
Fasting
Novenas
Apologetics
Graciousness when under fire
Trust through trials
Uniting sufferings to Christ's
Happiness in the next life
Detachment from this world
Love of enemies

CHAPTER 12

Small Groups, Big Blessings

"Do nothing from selfishness or conceit, but in humility
count others better than yourselves."
—Philippians 2:3

We had moved back to the suburbs of Austin, Texas, after our farm dream imploded and were attending a beautiful parish, St. William Catholic Church.

My wife and I had a good relationship with our parish priest, and we asked him what he most desired for the parish. He said that he wished we would start small groups of couples at the parish, because the parish was so big that people easily got lost and felt no connection with the community.

He explained that he would like the small couples groups to be ones where people would form strong bonds, which you often see in Protestant churches, especially Evangelical Protestant ones, that would help people to remain strong in their Catholic Faith and not get pulled away into Protestant churches that look like they offered a more enjoyable community.

Small Couples Group Begins

My wife and I were also feeling lonely during this time in our life as a couple and jumped at the chance to help out our parish while making good friends through the small group we would form.

We began exploring different formats that we thought could work, deciding that forming an adults-only group from couples would be the first step. The children would not attend the small group meetings and during the meetings the couples would come together for a potluck meal followed by a Bible study.

In this way, the small group would serve both as a means to fellowship and a way of more deeply learning our Catholic Faith.

We considered whether to meet at the parish or in people's homes, and ultimately decided that meeting in couples' homes was the best idea, because as soon as you involved the parish, there were many bureaucratic hurdles you had to jump through: reserving rooms, what you could and couldn't do in those rooms, who was certified for "Ethics and Integrity Ministry" (the program put in place by U.S. bishops to prevent sexual abuse), and so on.

My wife and I invited five couples that we knew to join us to pilot the first small group program at our parish. It was clear that there was a need and hunger that people at the parish had for a closer community, and we were glad to do our part to help fill that need.

Saintly Selflessness

As we began our group, Catherine and I had been reading about how the saints had always sought to fulfill the needs of others, selflessly, and not look to their own needs.

We were already practicing this to a degree by asking our priest what he wanted us to bring to his parish, but also in the small couples group, we opened up the format to input from the different couples, as they might have ideas that would help shape it and improve it.

We faced the temptation to claim credit for the small group idea, a temptation that would grow larger later on, but the saints did not operate in that way. They were not grasping, trying to take ownership of things in pride and vanity.

So we started our small group, and the first night went great. After discussing with the other couples, we decided to study a book of the Bible, and we bought a Bible study booklet that was Catholic. Each session we met at the home of one of the couples, ate dinner together, talked and laughed, and then we would do our study.

Friends in Need

About nine months into this pilot small group, my family and I encountered a serious situation, one that was incredibly difficult and stressful for us. But what happened next was unexpectedly wonderful. We turned to the couples in our small group for support, trusting that they would not reject us, and it was from these couples that we received the most help. They made us meals. They supported us emotionally. They babysat for us.

After a few months, by God's grace, we emerged from the crisis stronger than ever. We saw how integral the small group had been and wondered what would have happened had we never started it.

We returned to our small group with a renewed gusto, refining the small group formula each meeting, figuring out what worked well, what didn't, and how to balance the fun fellowship aspect with the faith formation. It was an iterative process, and some of the original ideas we thought would work, didn't, or had to be streamlined.

After several more months, Catherine and I announced that this pilot group was a success. We had been meeting for a full year and had ironed out the kinks in the program. Now we planned to start a second small group to prove out that the groups could multiply and grow.

Several of the couples in our group objected strongly to this decision. We had formed such a close bond together that they did not want our group to change or be broken up in any way.

While we understood their feelings and felt similarly, we reminded them that this group was not supposed to be just for us; rather, many people at our parish would benefit from having such a group. But we had to demonstrate a proven way that the groups could be formed and grow.

Multiplication, and Division

So we left the group, and we started a new one with another set of couples. Happily, our original group invited more couples to join their group to fill the hole that we had left, and their group continued to thrive.

Our new group went well, and after a year we went to our parish priest and told him that the small group concept would be a success if we followed the formula that we had been using. We shared with him the many blessings we had all received from it and how we envisioned rolling it out to the entire parish.

Our priest was delighted, and he told us that we could have all the Masses set up for announcements so that we could roll out this program to as many couples in the parish as wanted to have a small group.

I was feeling proud of what we were accomplishing, but then something happened that threatened to turn my pride on its head. We found out about the existence of another, competing couples program, one that was being piloted elsewhere in our diocese, and that our parish was considering using that program instead.

I felt this new program was a threat to all the work we did to design and refine the small group concept. We had worked hard at it, and now I had a protective feeling about it, and, if I were being honest, our status as founders.

I kept feeling a nagging suspicion. Maybe it was my conscience talking, but I had an inkling that I wasn't thinking as the saints would have thought.

Imitating the Saints

A friend of mine had given me an old book called *The Imitation of Christ*, which is a spiritual classic, second only to the Bible as one of the best-selling books of all time. I had read it when first becoming a Catholic, though its lessons were too advanced for me at the time.

Picking it up again, I hoped that I might find something in it that would help me know how to act. Should I fight to push our program into the parish and try to get them to not use the other one, or should I relax my grasp on it all and let God do what He wanted with the situation?

I ran across this passage, where the author said:

"Do not think yourself better than others lest, perhaps, you be accounted worse before God Who knows what is in man. Do not take pride in your good deeds, for God's judgments differ from those of men and what pleases them often displeases Him. If there is good in you, see more good in others, so that you may remain humble. It does no harm to esteem yourself less than anyone else, but it is very harmful to think yourself better than even one. The humble live in continuous peace, while in the hearts of the proud are envy and frequent anger."

Ouch. That hit home. I had felt anger about our program potentially being passed over in favor of the other one. My anger illuminated the pride living in my heart: pride at being recognized by others as the originator of this program. God was showing me a different way, the supernatural way of virtue: I needed to let go of the pride and ownership for the program and be at peace no matter which one the parish chose.

While thinking and praying about this, I remembered a verse in the Bible where St. Paul talked about humility. I looked it up and found it in Philippians 2:3, "Do nothing from selfishness or conceit, but in humility count others better than yourselves."

Count others as better than yourself. Now that's a concept I wasn't following here.

It rubbed against my grain, to be happy if someone else's creation was chosen over mine. But this was another secret ingredient that the saints employed to practice heroic virtue. And if it worked for them, I knew it would work for me.

The saints didn't clamor for credit. They actually would have been glad that someone else was chosen over them. So long as God was glorified and his people were helped by the work, they did not care who got the credit. They were truly selfless, and this is how we needed to be.

Catherine and I came to peace about the situation, and a week later, we received word that our parish had selected our program as the one they would use and that we had been chosen to lead the program. We had to decline though.

Here, Our Lord was giving us an extra dose of humility by taking away from us entirely the honor of getting to start the new program in our parish due to our daughter becoming very sick (which I'll share with you in the next chapter). This sickness came on right before we were going to launch the program parish-wide and required that we hand the reins over to another family in our new group to do the launch.

The outcome of it all: The small group program at our parish, launched by the other couple in our new group, was a success, and eleven new small groups of six couples each were started. Our own small group has continued to be a blessing to us, and we meet with them to this day.

Through this situation, I realized how tightly that I had been clutching the ownership of the program, wanting the credit for the idea. I realized how my actions had been prideful and vain. Our Lord showed me though that pride was not His way and not the way of the saints. Instead, God's way was that we should always do what is right and leave the results in His hands, with the credit going to whomever He desired.

How to Mix in This Ingredient

St. Andre Bessette was the unlikeliest man to become a saint. He was physically weak, wasn't a brilliant theologian, and multiple times he was almost expelled from the religious Order that he wanted to be in.

Ultimately, they decided he could do one job, be a doorman, and for the remaining forty years of his life that is what he did day-in and day-out. He was devoted to St. Joseph, and he asked the bishop if he could build a chapel to the saint. The bishop refused, citing that he did not want to borrow money and go into debt to build any such chapel.

So Andre, using the small change that he was paid to do haircuts at the boy's school where his religious Order worked, built a simple wooden shelter as the chapel. Over the subsequent decades, as soon as Andre saved up enough money, he would add on to the wooden chapel.

Eventually he was able to start building what he dreamed, a true basilica, but he died before he saw it fully completed. No matter, since all that he wanted was the chapel to be built in St. Joseph's honor, because of the great devotion he had to that saint.

Unassuming, humble, and faithful, Andre worked his whole life at the most basic jobs and started with what he had, ultimately taking no credit for the work that he did. Only in hindsight were people able to see how much his life blessed countless people.

Growing in selflessness is a lifelong task. You know how hard it is. We naturally want to get the credit, the praise, the applause, or the fame that goes with doing something great. But at the supernatural level, Jesus has told us that if we want to be great, we must be the servant of all.

And so, practicing that detachment from worldly things, including the human praise and credit for doing something good, we look for the opportunity to allow the credit to go to others instead of ourselves.

The Small Group Formula in Lionheart Catholic

Based on the information in this chapter, you could start a small couples group at your parish right now. It's quite simple: invite five other couples to start meeting together once per month at one of your houses, do it potluck style, and choose a book to read together that has spiritual value, so that you can discuss it.

But in Lionheart Catholic, I provide the step-by-step guide for starting such a group (or even multiple groups) at your parish. The great thing is, you can also interact directly with other Lionheart members who are starting their own small groups.

Small groups have been such a benefit for our family that I want every Catholic to experience them. Maybe God is calling you to start one where you are?

Okay, you have made it this far. Congratulations! You are over three-quarters of the way there, and yet some of the most essential ingredients are still yet to come.

I have saved one of the most powerful ingredients for the end, not because I am holding back on you, but simply because it took me almost twenty years to discover it myself. You, however, will be able to start practicing it right when you read it. The Vatican better get ready for a tidal wave of canonizations, starting with you!

The Recipe of the Saints

The Bible
Eucharistic Adoration
Catechism of the Catholic Church
The Rosary
The Theology of the Body
Aquinas's Virtue Principles
Fasting
Novenas
Apologetics
Graciousness when under fire
Trust through trials
Uniting sufferings to Christ's
Happiness in the next life
Detachment from this world
Love of enemies
Selfless humility

CHAPTER 13

A Princess in Peril

"We rejoice in our sufferings, knowing that suffering
produces endurance, and endurance produces character,
and character produces hope"
—Romans 5:3,4

Our family finally felt as if we were coming into a time of stability and calm. The lawsuit was over; we had made strong friendships in our small group; my job was in a good place, and our children were healthy.

One day our daughter Josephine, who had just turned four years old, fell and bumped her face on the floor. Over the next few days, we noticed that the fall had seemingly produced a lump on her cheek underneath her left eye, and we thought that she'd probably get a black eye from it.

A week went by, and she did not get a black eye; instead the lump swelled more, and when we touched it, it was firm to the touch. It seemed strange, so we decided to take her into the children's hospital in our city.

We went into the ER, and they did the normal stuff: taking blood, taking her temperature, and the doctor looked at the bump. She thought perhaps it was a little contusion or something like that, no big deal.

A Big Deal

About an hour went by, and the doctor had not come back into the room we were in. For such a routine injury, it seemed like quite a long time to figure out what was going on. At one point, I looked through the glass window in our ER room door and saw the pediatrician outside in the nurse's area, and she was looking at me with a very sober look on her face.

Another hour went by, and we began to wonder what was happening. Then a new doctor came in, and he said that there was something that showed up in Josephine's blood that indicated something very serious.

Then he delivered the worst news of our life: "I am sorry to tell you that your daughter has cancer."

Catherine and I stared at him in shock. We had gone into the ER expecting a routine bump, and instead Josephine had cancer. Our minds erupted with fears: what kind of cancer was it? Was it terminal? Could it be treated? What do we do now? What's going to happen to our daughter?

The doctor was a pediatric oncologist, and he explained that he did not yet know the answers to those questions but that they were already working on finding out, and we would start treatment as soon as possible.

"You're Aren't Going Anywhere"

I said to him, "Okay, well, we are ready to go home now. Please call us as soon as Josephine needs to begin treatment."

He said, "Oh no, you aren't going anywhere. You can't leave. She is going to be admitted into the oncology ward immediately where we will prepare her to get a port surgically implanted into her chest so that we can give chemo drugs through it."

Catherine and I felt trapped, as if we were held against our will and were falling into the belly of the beast. Our poor daughter was hungry and upset, but she was not allowed to eat anything because she had to fast before the anesthesia and immediate surgery.

We were admitted into the cancer ward, and in rooms all around us were sick children, many of whom were bald and had lost their hair, some of whom could not walk due to the chemo drugs wreaking havoc on their system, some with sunken eyes that looked sad and haunting.

The next eight days were a blur, as the doctors dumped information on us. A few days into our stay, the biopsy results came back, and our cancer doctor was relieved to tell us it was not the virulent form of cancer he had feared, but rather "only leukemia."

I didn't know what that worse form of cancer was that he had feared, but the word *leukemia* gave me chills. I knew children who had gotten leukemia and died from it, so hearing the word sent a bolt of terror through me.

My wife and I were both terrified, and we asked the doctor what the odds were that she would survive. I understand now that that was not a fair question to ask, that he could not know yet, but he gave us the assurance that they would do everything they could to find the best treatment that would give her best chance to survive.

High Intensity

A few weeks later, we were finally out of the hospital, and Josephine had received her first rounds of treatment. The cancer cells had been sent to the Mayo Clinic for analysis, and the results came back that the type of leukemia she had indicated that, even if the cancer went into remission, she would have a very high risk for relapse.

With this new--and alarming--information, her treatment changed immediately. The best chance for her now was a treatment that was pioneered by St. Jude's Children's Hospital, called the Total Fifteen Protocol. This treatment was very high intensity, in hopes of both knocking out the cancer but also preventing its relapse, but at increased risk that side effects of the chemo could cause severe and permanent damage to her organs and body.

My wife and I probed and peppered the doctor with questions: "Was this the *only* treatment option, the best treatment possible? Should we move to Nashville, and go to St. Jude's? Are we doing everything possible for her?"

We were full of fear at the thought of losing our daughter and also of the very real chance that the cure would be worse than the disease and permanently impair her. The fears descended upon us and consumed us. We did not want our daughter to see our fear though, because we knew that she needed us to be very strong so that she could be strong and fight against the cancer.

Doubts on Treatment

When we shared the treatment plan with a couple whom we had been close to for many years, they told us that they had been looking into alternative cancer treatments and that we should consider abandoning the doctor's plan and go with what they had learned.

They had studied these alternative treatments and found that many people had successfully treated their cancer with essential oils and intensive vitamin doses. They argued (justifiably) that the conventional cancer medicines were themselves carcinogenic (cancer-causing), so we were fighting fire with fire, and Josephine was the one getting burned.

Catherine and I were fairly "organic" in our approach to nutrition and the food we ate, and given Catherine's reservations about being stuck in the gears of the big medical machine, our friends' words gave us pause. Were we going to put our daughter at risk by submitting to this chemo treatment, especially one of very high intensity?

As an engineer, the biggest problem I had with the alternative treatments was that they had no scientifically validated studies done on them. All the success stories were anecdotal. While they may have been honest and true, we had no way to verify that vitamins and essential oils cured someone's cancer, and even if they did that they would also work on our daughter's specific kind of leukemia.

I wasn't willing to risk it. My daughter couldn't be the guinea pig for the alternative treatment movement. I thanked our friends for their well-intentioned suggestions but firmly insisted that we would not be going that route. They pressed the matter over the next few weeks, not taking "no" for an answer, and finally I bluntly blurted out that if *their* daughter got cancer, they could try out the alternative treatment. They stopped pushing after that.

After this point, Catherine and I came to harmony on the treatment plan. We no longer had arguments with the doctors but had the grace to accept that Josephine was receiving the best treatment available.

To Break or Unite

Over the following months, we met another family and got to know them. The wife was the one who normally took their son into the cancer clinic for treatment, and one day we spoke with her and asked how she and her husband were doing.

"Not well," she said quietly while her son was in the Infusion room getting his treatment. "My husband and I are divorcing."

Catherine and I were stunned into silence. She told us that the stress from the cancer treatments, the hospital stays, the sicknesses, had all been too much for her husband. She needed his help to keep the family going, but his work was already very demanding, and with the added pressure and responsibility from his son's cancer, he was pushed beyond his limit.

Catherine and I went home that day. I told her that I didn't want that to happen to us. She said she agreed, but then she told me that she was starting to get pushed beyond what she could endure, not because I wasn't helping a ton already, but because being in the clinic and hospital made her feel trapped and every time pushed her to the edge of panic attacks.

Catherine had been the one who would stay overnight with Josephine when she was admitted for days-long and weeks-long hospital stays. She asked me if I could be the one who stayed overnight on those in-patient visits.

In my mind, I wondered if I could juggle going from work directly to the hospital, staying overnight, then straight back to work and repeating it again, never going home for days or weeks. But if that--staying overnight--was what it would take, I wanted to do it.

I learned a secret of the saints through deciding to give up my schedule and my sleep so that I could be with my daughter and give my wife a rest: I had to release control over my routine, do my best with the situation as it came, and leave the results in God's hands. This was what the saints did. And now I was starting to do it.

I told Catherine that I would take the overnight shifts and prayed for strength of high Heaven to help me. The next in-patient visit was coming up. We implemented our new roles, with me coming to the hospital right after work and staying overnight, then going into the office directly from the hospital when Catherine came in the morning to be with Josephine.

That week felt like a blur for me, especially since the nurses had to come into the hospital room every few hours, check Josephine's vitals, change out the medicines going into her body through her chest port, so she and I never got good sleep. By the end of that five-day stay, I was wiped out and exhausted. But we had done it.

Through these times together, Josephine and I became very close. One day when I was in the bathroom of our hospital room while she was receiving treatment, I overhead the doctor ask Josephine what she liked most about me. Josephine said, "My daddy always helps me."

My eyes filled with tears, and my heart overflowed with gratitude to God. I may not be a hero to anyone else, but I was a hero to my daughter.

I continued going to all the overnight hospital stays, helping my heroic wife to not burn out, to not be induced into panic attacks. She had given so much, and God had to give me the strength to give more.

Over the next six months, we perfected this system. Through it, we both came to love and appreciate each other more than we ever thought possible. Instead of being torn apart, like the one couple had so tragically been, we were united even more closely together.

Through this time, Catherine also learned this same secret of the saints: we had to release control, do our very best, and leave the results in God's hands.

The Long Haul

Josephine continued going to the hospital both for the various treatments and because, with her compromised immune system, she was prone to getting fevers and illnesses that could be dangerous to her.

All her hair fell out. She began a new medicine, one that could damage her eyes severely and another one that could damage her heart. She started developing hives in reaction against some of the medicines, but the worst was seeing the emotional toll that the treatment and the pain was inflicting upon her.

Her little heart was internally bearing the burdens of a weak immune system, frequent fevers and illnesses due to it, her stomach hurting almost all the time from the different medicines, and nausea.

She began to lose weight, something that the doctor said was common but that we had to control so that she did not get too weak. There were moments when I looked into her eyes and saw glimpses of the haunted dullness we had seen in the eyes of the other children that first week in the cancer ward.

But through it all, she remained our little trooper, and Edmund her older brother was as well.

All these treatments culminated in one truly great day, the day when the doctors gave us the news we'd craved: Josephine's leukemia was in full remission!

And after three long years, the treatment was finally finished. Josephine's hair grew back; her little body began to heal, and her immune system began to recover. Josephine emerged from the treatment with an inner strength of iron. Due to the suffering she had endured, she was mature beyond her years. Going into treatment, she had had a best friend who was the same age. Now they were at such different maturity levels that they could barely play together.

Through this experience, I let go completely of the need I had to protect her. Leukemia was something I could not shield her from. No one could. God allowed her to suffer from her sickness, and that was something I had to accept.

Life, all life, was in His hands. My children were in His hands. They belonged to Him. My role, then, was to help them on their way to Heaven (and I myself wanted to not lose Heaven, either, so I could be with them in eternity).

St. Louis, King of France, had a family motto: "Anything but a mortal sin." It became my motto too, for only a mortal sin could exclude me from Heaven and prevent me from being with my daughter if God were to take her.

Through this difficult chapter, I resolved all the more to strive to be a saint, to follow our Lord, and to help my children always stay close to Him in sanctifying grace.

How to Mix in This Ingredient

This ingredient is another one that you don't have to go searching for. Rather, God will bring you into situations where you need to release control, do your best, and leave the results in God's hands.

Mother Teresa has a famous quote which summarizes this ingredient well: "God did not call me to be successful, but to be faithful." Success may be the result, but that result is what we leave to God's providence. Being faithful means we are doing our best to bring about success while releasing the outcome, releasing control to Him.

If you think for even a few seconds, you will be able to think of a problem in your life that you know you need to release to God. If you're drawing a blank, do what I do: simply look at what you are currently worried about, both big and small. Those worries are the opportunities for you to do your best, while releasing control and leaving the results in God's hands.

Maybe for you it is the worry that your children will leave the Catholic Faith. Or the fear that, having left the Faith, they will never return to it. Maybe it is a fear that your long-term job prospects are poor, and that you will not be able to provide for your family. Whatever it is, give control of it to God, and simply do your best each day with it.

The Recipe of the Saints

The Bible
Eucharistic Adoration
Catechism of the Catholic Church
The Rosary
The Theology of the Body
Aquinas's Virtue Principles
Fasting
Novenas
Apologetics
Graciousness when under fire
Trust through trials
Uniting sufferings to Christ's
Happiness in the next life
Detachment from this world
Love of enemies
Selfless humility
Release control, do your best, and leave the results in God's hands

CHAPTER 14

The Father's Embrace

"Having purified your souls by your obedience to the
truth for a sincere love of the brethren, love one another
earnestly from the heart."
—1 Peter 1:22

Now, we entered into a calm season. We had come through
a farm that flopped, severe back pain and surgery, getting
sued, and our daughter getting leukemia.

My children were still young but growing fast. A friend
of mine shared a great quote with me about family life that
epitomized this time: "The days go by slowly, but the years go
by quickly."

I wanted to rear my children to be healthy, happy, and holy.
I wanted them to follow our Lord, because from making bad
choices in my own life for many years, I had realized that following God was the wisest thing to do, that His way was the
best way. I wanted to help them to see that.

We had some challenges though. Our daughter was still
struggling with the emotional consequences of three years
from fighting leukemia, and our son had some unique emotional challenges as well.

Children Abandoning the Faith

When I became Catholic as a young, single man, I was blessed with a mentor. I looked up to him and watched closely over the years as he and his wife reared their many children. They went to daily Mass, prayed the Rosary regularly, said prayers before meals, and were just generally devout.

Fast forward ten years later, and I looked on with dismay as their eldest children became teenagers, graduated from high school and left the house, only to also leave the Catholic Faith entirely.

His children embraced a vague agnosticism and quit going to Mass, rejecting their faith completely. In spite of this disturbing pattern, I held out hope for his younger daughter, who had always been really special, and who I thought was still practicing her faith.

This daughter, now out in the working world, sent us wedding invitation. I was excited to open it, only to read with sadness that she was not getting married in the Church at all but at a resort. No sacrament, no wedding Mass, no Bible readings, no priest.

I began to ponder what I had observed in the years of close friendship with this dad, since he had often invited me to family gatherings and welcomed me into his family's life.

Toxic Culture

One observation I made was that this father was very trusting of society, and he wanted his children to not seem strange, so he let them imbibe a lot of pop culture. I remember when his teenage son started listening to Tupac Shakur and gangster rap music all the time like his friend's buddies were; his father allowed this, wanting his son to be socially acceptable.

I silently disagreed with him letting his children drink in the dregs of our toxic culture, but this dad was fifteen years older than I and had mentored me in my Catholic faith, so I did not feel that I had the wisdom to offer him a correction.

Another aspect was at play as well. While this father himself had been converted to the Catholic Faith and was a practicing Catholic, he did not communicate to his children how deeply his faith was part of his life. Instead, he came across as aloof from his faith, detached rather than warm and affectionate. In short, he did not authentically portray how his faith was intrinsic to his very being.

Saintly Warmth

Watching my friend's children abandon God emphasized to me what was at stake. It stoked in me my burning desire to do everything I could to win my children's hearts for Christ and His Church. Needing a model, I pondered who I could imitate, someone who practiced that essential warmth and authenticity with children. I came across St. John Bosco.

St. John Bosco grew up in Italy in a poor peasant family in the early 1800s. He had remarkable adeptness of mind, and from an early age was given a vision from God that he would reach the hearts of young people in his life.

At twelve years of age, he began to hear God calling him to the priesthood. But his family had little money and could not afford seminary education. Through hard work and a providential meeting with Father (now Saint) Joseph Cafasso, he was able to attend seminary and become a priest.

Don Bosco, as he affectionately became known, was immediately drawn to helping the many children in need. He attracted their attention through all sorts of means, including simple magic tricks and sleights of hand, but then once they were intrigued, he warmly shared with them his great love of Jesus Christ, and how they could love God as well.

He became the spiritual father to hundreds, then thousands of children and young people, helping them discover Christ, find their vocations, find good jobs, and to lead happy lives.

God made him a father to many, and God the Father loved these children through Don Bosco's warmth and authenticity. I realized that this was who I wanted to imitate with my children.

Don Bosco was genuine and human, and the people who found themselves in his presence immediately grasped this and so were drawn to God, from whom this goodness came. I resolved to be warm, affectionate, and authentic in demonstrating to my children how much I loved them and our Catholic Faith, how essential it was to my very life and being on a daily basis.

I also resolved to present the Faith in a compelling and attractive way, showing it to be so much greater and better than what the culture offered. I knew that there was to be a war for my children's souls. The toxic culture would present something very alluring, glitzy, fun, promising all the pleasure that they could want with no consequences and no responsibilities, something that is ultimately empty.

I needed to counter this toxic lie, present the truth to them, and present it in a way that would help them see beyond the falsehoods of the toxic culture and see that the truth, beauty, and goodness was found in their Catholic Faith.

Revelations

During one of our small couples group meetings, I was speaking with the other dads in the group, asking them what they thought about how we could share our faith with our children so that they would not leave the Church (as my mentor dad's children had done).

During the conversation that followed, one of my friends said, "My wife's been telling me that I need to show affection for our children, but I don't know how to. My parents, especially my father, we're not affectionate toward me. We didn't hug. We didn't give kisses on the cheek. My father didn't do anything like that with me."

Encouraged by this confession, one of the other dads in our group admitted the same thing. He didn't know how to be affectionate with his children. I was able to share with them how simple it was to be affectionate, and so was one of the other dads in the group, who had warm, affectionate parents.

We explained that it just simple gestures: a hug here and there, doing a little wrestling together, snuggling together, having your child sit on your knee while you read them a story, small things done frequently on a daily basis that helped to build that affectionate connection.

These other dads expressed doubt that they could do this in a way that would come across as natural and normal. I told them that at first it might feel forced to them, but by just practicing it over time, it would become more natural, and their children's responses could guide the dads to the ways of affections that most resonated with the children.

I so longed for my friends to be able to keep their children Catholic, just as I hoped to do with my children.

Prudent Friendships

We noticed another problem with several of our friends whose children had left the Faith. They had let their children be friends with many other children who were not Catholic.

While in some cases this is just fine, in others we noticed that these friends were not good influences on their children and exposed them to hyper-sexualized music and hedonistic ideas, images and ideas young children are not ready for.

For my wife and I, we decided early on that we wanted to homeschool and keep our children out of the public school system. My wife and I were both products of the public school system and great successes with it, but as adults we realized that one of the purposes of public school was indoctrination into the secular American culture.

While homeschooling has not been easy, we have stuck with it. Our children get lots of social time with the neighbors on our street, some of whom are Catholic, as well as through the various sports and civic activities that we participate in as a family. But we are careful in how we guard our children's friendships and in what they are exposed to.

What we have seen from following this plan is that our children have grown closer to us than ever. They have seen that following the Catholic Faith leads to good results, whereas rejecting God's plan leads to bad outcomes. They've witnessed first-hand that doing things God's way is the best way.

The fruit of our efforts with our children has been evident in the trust they show us. On multiple occasions at night when we are tucking the children into their beds, they have shared with us experiences that frightened them or upset them. Some of these experiences were truly concerning, and we never would have known about them had they not felt the trust to share with us.

For example, one time while playing a kid's game on his grandmother's tablet computer, my son told me that an image of a woman popped up that he didn't understand. We talked through it, and I told the grandparent what had happened. Of course, she was deeply disturbed. Wanting to find out why this pornographic image had appeared on a children's game, I did some research. I found out that a rash of "children's apps" had made it into the app store, loaded with pornographic images. Sick and vicious, but that is the kind of thing that happens today in our society.

Catherine and I felt greatly blessed that our children have revealed this and other happenings to us. Thanks be to God, I've become a father like I never imagined I'd be: loving, faithful, and warm, all thanks to God and to my wife who has taught me many ways I can be a better parent.

Time and time again she would offer me a gentle suggestion for how I could change the way that I acted, avoiding anger with the children, and being more like our Father in Heaven. I went from despising children and being afraid of them as an atheist, to now being so grateful that God blessed me with two children and showed me, one lesson at a time, how I could best parent my children with their own unique needs and give the very best chance that they would remain Catholic.

How to Mix in This Ingredient

Warmth, affection, and authenticity come more naturally to some parents than they do to others.

That said, you can grow in these virtues. So even if your parents were not especially affectionate with you, and even if you grew up in a home that was not even Catholic, you can learn how your own family can be different.

I like to learn by imitation. There are certain dads that I have looked up to or appreciated as I watched how they interacted with their children. Maybe they are wise, or prudent, or have some particular manner with their children that I really like and see the good effects of.

I will observe these fathers, see what they are doing, and then try to imitate them with my own children. Now, every dad is different, and sometimes you have to adapt what another person does so that it fits with your own personality and the personalities of your children, but there is no shame in simply copying the good practices that someone else is doing.

Authenticity, in particular sharing your Catholic Faith with your children in a way that comes across as sincere and real, is difficult or impossible to fake. What that means is that you want to endeavor to grow strong in your own faith, to understand what it teaches, and how to live a truly Catholic life, so that when you are sharing your faith with your children, it will be authentic.

You've probably heard before that children have a "hypocrisy radar" that's very strong. They know when their mother or father is not practicing what they preach. Sometimes this is more obvious, for instance when a dad who is not Catholic nonetheless goes to Mass with his family week in and week out, but never receives the Eucharist.

Children see their dad is not taking part, does not really believe any of it, and those actions, more than anything that their dad might say, will have a dramatic influence on whether his children remain Catholic or not.

The closer that we get to God, the closer we get to becoming the saints that He has designed us to be, and every saint was warm and authentic. The falsity and pretension have been stripped away through the practice of virtue and a life of prayer.

We can have that too. That is the purpose of this book and also why I have started Lionheart Catholic, to bring Catholics together who want to live differently, to rear their children to remain in the Faith, to renew the Church from within, and to transform the world.

The Recipe of the Saints

The Bible
Eucharistic Adoration
Catechism of the Catholic Church
The Rosary
The Theology of the Body
Aquinas's Virtue Principles
Fasting
Novenas
Apologetics
Graciousness when under fire
Trust through trials
Uniting sufferings to Christ's
Happiness in the next life
Detachment from this world
Love of enemies
Selfless humility
Release control, do your best, and leave the results in
God's hands
Warm authenticity

CHAPTER 15

Praying Like the Saints

"But when you pray, go into your room and shut the door
and pray to your Father who is in secret; and your Father
who sees in secret will reward you."
—Matthew 6:6

Early in my Catholic journey, I heard about "meditation." Attempting to learn more, I read some articles about meditation online, and I came away from my reading believing that the type of meditation Catholics were supposed to do was called centering prayer.

So I started practicing centering prayer. I would go to my room, close my eyes, and attempt to silence my mind. I was told that while doing centering prayer, if thoughts came into my mind that were not something I wanted, I should hold the thought for a moment while saying to myself, "this thought is not mine," and then dismiss it.

Catholic Buddhism?

The practice of centering prayer struck me as a little odd, because as an atheist, I had dabbled lightly in Buddhism, and while learning about Buddhism, I had tried to do Buddhist meditation: staring at a candle flame and attempting to empty my mind of all thoughts and desires.

When thoughts or desires came into my mind doing this Buddhist meditation, I would "feed them" into the flame, to try to "form the void" in my mind. This practice of emptying my mind of thoughts and rejecting any that came in was exactly what I was doing in centering prayer. It felt like Eastern mysticism, just with a splash of Christianity washed over it.

After many months of doing centering prayer, I found articles that explained that centering prayer was not authentically Catholic and not what Catholic meditation was at all, that it was more like Eastern mysticism and dangerous.

This confirmed my intuition, and I gave up the practice. Unfortunately, I now associated the word meditation with centering prayer and Eastern mysticism, so I wanted to have nothing to do with those practices.

Hitting a Spiritual Plateau

Over the next fifteen years, I did my best to grow in my faith as a Catholic. I dutifully went to Mass on Sundays and holy days of obligation, prayed the Rosary fairly frequently, as well as other prayers like novenas.

Nonetheless, I realized I had been confessing the same handful of sins--one of which was giving into excessive anxiety--again and again. Anxiety seemed to be my predominant fault, and I had hit a ceiling spiritually and did not know how to break through it.

I knew that God wanted me to become a saint, but deep in my heart I didn't think it was possible. Oh, maybe it was possible for a few special people, and God gave them miraculous graces that let them do amazing things, and be heroically virtuous, but I was now well into my second decade as a Catholic, and I did not seem to be making any progress in becoming a saint.

"What if God did not really make it possible for me to be a saint?" I thought. What if I was simply too selfish and lazy?

Real Catholic Meditation

Then one day I watched a YouTube video by a priest, talking about meditation. At first, I was very much on guard because of my previous experience with centering prayer. But as I listened, I learned that the meditation he was talking about was something quite different from the centering prayer I had been exposed to.

The priest called this meditation "mental prayer," and the purpose of it was not to empty yourself of all thoughts or desires but rather to encounter the loving God. So, instead of filling yourself with emptiness, as I had tried with Buddhist meditation and centering prayer, you were asking to be "filled" by God's love.

I learned from this priest that all the saints had practiced mental prayer. That fact surprised me and piqued my curiosity. Attempting to corroborate this claim, I ran across this quote from St. Alphonsus Liguori: "Every saint became a saint through mental prayer."

So not only did the saints practice mental prayer, it was *the* way that they became saints! I felt elated at this discovery. I had uncovered a key ingredient that all the saints knew about but which I had never heard a homily on in my life.

Additionally, I found out that there were multiple levels of prayer, with vocal prayer being the first and most basic level.

Mental prayer was the second level, but there were levels beyond even this, that we could rise to.

Well, the only way to make it up a stairwell is by going one step at a time, so I started doing five minutes of mental prayer per day. I went to a quiet room, shut the door, closed my eyes, and chose a particular topic to meditate upon.

As I meditated upon the topic, thoughts and emotions arose in my heart: sometimes contrition and sorrow for sin, sometimes gratitude to our Lord for His love for me and my family, sometimes appreciation for Christ's Church and how He has guided her.

I would offer these thoughts and emotions (called "affections" in the parlance of mental prayer) to God, and typically that led to me thinking about persons and situations that were on my heart to pray for, and I would offer to God prayers of petition for myself, for things I hoped to happen, for other people in my life. I learned that making such requests to God during mental prayer was not only ok, but an intrinsic part of it.

At the end of the meditation, I would make a resolution to overcome my predominant fault, which was excessive anxiety, and I would make a commitment to defeat it in some concrete way.

A Wandering Mind

Each day, when doing my meditation, I found it difficult to endure the five minutes of quiet. Unless I committed to doing it everyday, I would put it off and then not do it, so I had to force myself to engage in mental prayer for those five minutes everyday.

During the meditation, my mind would wander all over, I would think about things that happened during the day, or a person who had irritated me and how angry I was at them, or I would be worried about something that was coming up or that I feared would happen. It was very difficult to focus.

I felt like I was wasting my time, and that this was just one more thing that was not going to work, one more thing that maybe some saints were given the grace to do, but that wasn't for me. In fact I saw no obvious benefit for months, and many days during my meditation I felt like I had done nothing at all, had made no progress, and was simply going through the motions.

Should I give up doing mental prayer? Was I doing it wrong, and was it going to be impossible for me to figure out, because I had no one to teach me?

I decided to plow on ahead though, because I believed that the saints all practiced this form of prayer, and they had not once led me astray. Every single ingredient that I had learned from the saints had been valuable in my spiritual life, and if mental prayer was the second level of prayer, after eighteen years as a Catholic, I had better start learning it.

Breakthrough

I stuck with it, and as Lent began, I increased the time to ten minutes per day.

I had now been doing mental prayer for a year, and to my delight, I began to see improvement in my confessions, because for the first time in a decade I had to confess *different* sins. I felt exhilarated that I was actually making progress on my predominant faults, ones that had been dominating my spiritual life for so long.

But I also I felt angry, even cheated, that never once had I heard a priest talk about mental prayer: what it was, how to do it, let alone that every Catholic should practice it in order to become a saint. It seemed as if this was one of those traditional practices where the baby was thrown out with the bathwater around the mid-twentieth century. It is a travesty, an injustice to all Catholics that this way of prayer has not been taught widely. It took me stumbling across some priest on YouTube for me to find out about it.

Through mental prayer, and the progress that I am now making in my spiritual life, I realize that God does make it possible for us to become saints, even someone as lazy, selfish, and anxious as I am. With God's help I can conquer my predominant faults. I can grow strong in virtue and become a saint, not by my own power, but by God's grace, through practicing mental prayer and the resolutions to live virtuously that blossom from it.

This secret ingredient has unlocked many more graces that I now cannot imagine living without. I've shared this "secret" with so many of my friends and family, wanting them to come to the same realization that I did, so that they can become saints as well. I even shared it with the small couples group that we are in, and we chose a book to read about mental prayer, and now every couple in our group is starting to practice mental prayer.

I imagine the Church, where every Catholic knows about mental prayer, talks about it, and learns from each other's discoveries, renewing the Church from within, and making great saints in the process.

How to Mix in This Ingredient

"Every saint became a saint through mental prayer." If that is not the best recommendation that I could give you for starting to practice mental prayer, I don't know what is.

But how do you do mental prayer? I'm going to give you the basic steps, so that you can begin today.

Meditation is silent prayer to God. It is turning your heart to God and allowing Him to move in you. Get started with five minutes per day. Prepare yourself by going to a quiet place, mentally placing yourself in God's presence, making the sign of the cross, and praying for the grace to meditate.

The second step is where you will reflect, by choosing a specific subject to meditate on. This subject could be any number of Catholic truths: how wonderful Heaven is; how fearful hell is; Jesus' Passion and death, or His Resurrection; some virtue of the saints; something you read in the Bible, or some truth of our Faith.

The third step is called affections. Affections, in this usage, are thoughts and feelings that will arise in your heart from reflecting on the subject that you've chosen. For instance, you might feel sorrow for sin as you're meditating upon Jesus' death on the Cross.

Or, if the topic is the Resurrection, you might feel hope and a desire to be with God in Heaven arise within you. Allow those affections, those emotions and thoughts, to percolate in you as you pray.

The fourth step, which normally arises in a natural way, is petitions. As you're doing your meditation, in silence you can bring prayer requests to God. It might be that someone you love is placed on your heart, and you know that they are in need in some way. Or it may be that you have a need that you need to pray for. You can and should bring those prayers to God in the quiet of your heart during mental prayer.

The fifth step is resolution. It is likely that you have a predominant fault or main vice that you struggle with in your life. It is very helpful to make some sort of concrete resolution or commitment that will help you to overcome this fault and grow in the opposite virtue. For instance, maybe lust is a sin you struggle with, and you make a resolution against lust and toward growing in purity.

These are the five steps, quite simple, to practice mental prayer. Note that these are the mechanics of it. You do not need to be rigidly bound to them; instead, you should let our Lord move in your heart and mind during the time of mental prayer as He so wills.

It might be that God moves you in one way or another, that some of the steps are out of order, or that some of the steps don't happen every time. That is fine. The steps provide a guide, a tool to help you to get into the right frame of mind, and they provide a structure so that in those times when you are distracted, you have something to follow that gives an order to how you're praying.

The most important thing by far is simply to commit to a certain amount of time per day and then do your best to practice mental prayer during that time. As the months go by, I recommend increasing the time you're praying from five to ten minutes. Now, you could always break that up into two five-minute blocks over the course of your day. It's up to you. And then, simply follow as our Lord leads you, to increase the time from there. My goal is to get up to thirty minutes per day, but I'm not there yet. Baby steps!

Those are the basic steps to practice mental prayer. You should start it today. But know that there is much more that you can learn about it that will accelerate your prayer life. To go deeper about how to do mental prayer and talk with others who are on the same journey with it, check out the Lionheart Catholic community.[6]

---

6   https://lionheartcatholic.com

Mental prayer is something I have still never heard a priest talk about from the pulpit in all the thousands of homilies that I've heard. It seems that it's been largely forgotten in the Church during this time, which is a woeful shame.

But, one person at a time, we will bring it back. Your time starts today!

The Recipe of the Saints

The Bible
Eucharistic Adoration
Catechism of the Catholic Church
The Rosary
The Theology of the Body
Aquinas's Virtue Principles
Fasting
Novenas
Apologetics
Graciousness when under fire
Trust through trials
Uniting sufferings to Christ's
Happiness in the next life
Detachment from this world
Love of enemies
Selfless humility
Release control, do your best, and leave the results in God's hands
Warm authenticity
Mental Prayer

CHAPTER 16

The Brotherhood

"But I have prayed for you that your faith may not fail; and
when you have turned again, strengthen your brethren."
—Luke 22:32

In my first five years as a Catholic, I had fought against addiction to pornography, and by God's grace I had conquered it, growing strong, especially in the virtue of purity.

During that time, I had occasion to talk to different Catholic guys about pornography addiction. I shared with them my own personal story of overcoming it, to offer them hope that they could too, along with the tools I used that the Church offered to defeat this evil.

Help Your Brothers

I was involved with my parish's men's group, a weekly meeting of men at the parish where we would watch a recorded video series from some Catholic priest or speaker. During one of these men's group meetings, a priest said that 80% of the men at his parish confess pornography addiction and masturbation.

The number did not surprise me, for I knew how prevalent this sin was, especially among men.

I felt a desire, perhaps a calling from God, I thought, to do something to help my brothers in Christ to overcome this vice. One idea that I began to develop was to start a different men's group at the parish, one focused on growing in purity. I came up with the structure for the meetings, topics we would discuss, how we would do the discussion and encourage each other, and then I went to my parish priest to propose this new group.

Parish Bureaucracy

Our parish was the biggest in the diocese, so big that it had a staff of around thirty full-time employees, including several directors and even a chief operating officer.

Because our parish was so big, I was told that I first had to make an appointment with the employee who did volunteer coordination. So I met with him, and he wanted me to go through a "discernment process" about whether this new group was a good idea, whether I was fit to lead such a group, and also where it would fit in his "four categories of ministry."

So I spent months filling out worksheets, meeting with him, and trying to get the group off the ground. I explained to him that the need for this was great, and that everyone knew that it was. This sin was the "elephant in the room" that people didn't want to talk about, and that my biggest fear was that people would be too afraid to come to the group. We needed to advertise it and promote it so that people would become aware that it existed and how it could help them.

Finally, I got provisional approval to start the group on a "trial" basis. But the parish bureaucracy was too afraid to advertise it, so at the first meeting only one other man came.

Undaunted, I continued on and made a web page on my own website to list when and where the group met each month, since my parish refused to add a webpage on their site for it.

Somehow, the parish bureaucrats found out about my webpage, and they called me to a meeting, confronting me about it, accusing me of making my webpage look like I was affiliated with the parish, since I linked to the parish's main website. I was embarrassed for them, as they did not seem to understand the basic way that websites worked and what it meant to simply link from one site to another.

They said that my webpage had caused a big problem and that I would have to take it down or risk getting my group's provisional approval permanently revoked. I agreed, but I requested that they add a simple webpage to the parish site that listed who our group was, what we were about, and when and where we met. They agreed, but weeks later, still there was no webpage.

Months went by, and only one or two men would come to the purity group meetings that I held. I kept asking the parish staff, including the "Communications Director," whose job it was to update the parish website, why they had not yet added the simple webpage to the site. I did not hear back, even after messaging them over and over.

Eventually a webpage was added, but that was all the advertising that would be done they said. Only once we graduated out of "provisional" status as a ministry could we receive a blurb in the bulletin, or any mention from the pulpit during announcements at Mass.

I felt extremely frustrated by the bureaucracy of the parish, which didn't seem to be focused on actually helping the people at the parish grow in holiness, but rather more about dotting the i's and crossing the t's with their forms and guidelines.

Facing Criticism

Around the same time, two friends of mine, one of whom had a business helping men to conquer pornography, reviewed the materials that I had developed, and I had asked them to give me input on them hoping for some good feedback.

To my surprise and chagrin, they each told me that I was wrong in my whole approach, that I would not help anyone to conquer pornography, and that I might even hurt them by giving them false hope that "my way" could help them in this.

I was dismayed, as "my way" was simply the Church's teachings and the means that the Church gave us to conquer this sin. There was nothing unique about what I was saying; rather, I was simply presenting my testimony of how following Christ and His Church had worked for me.

Both friends said that I was not getting to the root of the problem and claimed that growing in virtue was only a surface-level change in behavior that would simply cause a relapse into sin later. Further, they said that novenas and scapulars and sacramentals did not work, that learning self-mastery in one virtue wouldn't help any with the virtue of purity. They claimed that a particular kind of change of heart, one that came from following the programs that *they* had developed, was the only way to defeat this sin.

I agreed with them that a change of heart was needed but told them that there was not just one way to bring that about. Nonetheless, their criticisms disheartened me. What if they were right, and the approach that I was offering was no good?

This was made all the more difficult because one of my strengths is known as "input." The strength of input means I like to hear what others think and to gather information (input) to take it into account for a better perspective and a better solution.

Gaining input is good, but the negative side of it is that when I receive conflicting input, like this criticism, it can make me feel paralyzed. And I did feel paralyzed. I had put a lot of work and time into making this program, so I was invested in it, but I didn't want to let that influence me in objectively evaluating whether my program was helpful or not.

I brought this conundrum to our Lord in my time of mental prayer for many weeks. I asked Him if what He had shown me and what the Church offered was still relevant to helping men today. I did not receive a direct answer from God. Instead, I came across St. Joan of Arc.

A French Peasant Girl Shows the Way

I had known about St. Joan of Arc for a long time, even watched a movie about her life. But now I dug into what had actually happened in the events of her life. She was a French peasant girl, a teenager, and God miraculously called her to lead an army and set things to rights for her country. A peasant girl leading an army!

Talk about unheard-of. In spite of strong opposition at every turn, she persevered in following the direction that God had given to her. She refused to let naysayers and doubters, and even opposing enemy forces, stop her from God's mission.

Ultimately, she was captured and shamefully tried in a kangaroo court presided over by, of all people, a Catholic bishop. Though she had no theological education, through her simple piety she evaded the traps set up by her inquisitors. They asked her if she knew she was in a state of sanctifying grace, and she answered: "If I am not, may God put me there; and if I am, may God so keep me."

This answer was brilliant, because if she had said "yes I know I am in a state of grace," they would have claimed she committed the sin of presumption, as no one, short of a private revelation, can know with certainty whether they are in a state of grace.

Nonetheless, her accusers condemned her to death for claiming, truthfully, that God had given her these visions and spoken to her in miraculous ways. St. Joan of Arc followed our Lord even in the face of ridicule and contradiction, remaining faithful to the vision and truth our Lord had given to her.

Staying True to the Vision

I felt confirmed in what our Lord had shown me with conquering lust, but I also incorporated some good aspects that I mined out from my friends' criticism. Even more so, I made my program one that doesn't claim to be the end-all-be-all but instead is more like a guide that leads men to various programs and resources, almost a directory of what Catholic men can use to find help.

The video course that I developed with my old friend Gerardo shared many of the secret ingredients of the saints that you have been learning in this book. But I also made videos on specific strategies for overcoming lust: how to interrupt the temptation right when it starts, before it can get too strong; how to affirm the beauty of women as manifestations of God's majestic beauty, without lusting; how to connect with intensive retreats that specifically help men grow in purity, and many more proven tactics.

The parish bureaucrats, meanwhile, kept the group from leaving provisional status, and they refused to share it with the parish. I spent hours trying to jump through their hoops, placating them, explaining it again to them, urging them of the need. I felt like giving up after months of this runaround. "If you don't want this," I said to myself, "why am I killing myself trying to bring it to you?"

At this point, one of the deacons at the parish who had just learned about my program, and who directed the parish's marriage prep program for couples, told me that there was a man who had come to him on the brink of divorce. "Can he come to your group?" he asked.

I said yes, and the man came to the next group meeting, telling us that due to impurity and pornography, he was on the brink of divorce with his wife. I worked with him closely; we were talking everyday, trying to save his marriage.

Unfortunately, his marriage ended in divorce. I felt upset that it was "too little, too late" to help him, but then a few months later, another man found our group and came to our meeting.

Vindication

This man was also in a bad way. To put it bluntly, it was a miracle that his wife was still with him. I offered the help that I could but also realized he needed something more, that he needed a group with whom he could meet everyday, something like a 12-step program that Alcoholics Anonymous uses.

I knew about a 12-step program just like this in our city, for sex addicts, this one run by a Protestant church. Even though it was Protestant-led, I knew that this Catholic man needed it, and I told him he should go to it.

A few months later, he came back and told me about his miraculous turnaround. He was elated with happiness and gratitude, because through this intensive 12-step program, he had finally turned the corner and was beginning to overcome the horrible addiction to lust that plagued him his whole adult life and throughout his marriage.

The approach that I was promoting, that of bringing all possible forces to bear on the problem, as well as connecting people in need with other groups and strategies, had paid off. I felt vindicated because of this man's success.

I realized that incorporating other people's perspectives was a great thing to do, but even more so was sticking to the vision that God had given to me, trusting that it was wise and right because the Church taught it.

My deep fear had been that my conquering lust had been a fluke. Maybe I was really just repressing this disorder within myself and was thus not truly free, which is what my friends accused me of. That fear, I realized, was unfounded, because not only had I defeated lust through following my plan, but through it other men were overcoming lust as well. You can't argue with results.

God made us all differently. There is no one magic key that works the same for every man to overcome this habitual sin. Rather, for one man, a particular devotion or prayer is the most effective, but for a different man, something different works.

So the best route, and the one I counseled men to try, was to throw the kitchen sink at the problem, to try many different approaches that the Church offers. Use all the weapons that God has given to us, and see what works best for you at the particular time and point where you are in your struggle.

Amazingly, when I put the program online, several groups around the country signed up for it and started their own small groups of Catholic men. I received feedback from them on the course and continued to refine it and improve it.

So I learned to trust in what God has shown me. People can share their opinions, but these opinions are not always founded on wisdom. Sometimes they come from erroneous understandings, simple mistakes, or even envy and jealousy. And sometimes multiple good ways exist to address a problem. It is a difficult balance to strike, but I am happy to say that the program, called "The Brotherhood of Virtue," has now helped scores of men around the country, and new groups continue to spring up.

The joy of being freed from slavery to sin is immense, and I want every man, especially every Catholic man, to have that experience. I know now that God can heal any person of this addiction; He is the Father who keeps His promises.

How to Mix in This Ingredient

This one is for the Catholic men. You can start a Brotherhood of Virtue small group program for purity for men at your parish. I'm going to give you the basic outline for how to do it right here, but for the full program, and the coaching and support that goes along with it, you'll find it in Lionheart Catholic.[7]

Starting a group focused on purity at your parish is a noble endeavor. The problem is so rampant and pervasive, that men need all the help that they can get, and the Church offers them powerful tools. If you do think God is leading you to start such a group, first meet with the parish priest and make sure that he is supportive of the endeavor. Explain to him that the purpose of the group is to help men conquer lust and pornography ad-

---

7   https://lionheartcatholic.com

diction, grow in purity, and also to protect their children and family from falling into this evil.

With his support, you can set a launch day when the first meeting will be held and also ask for permission to submit a bulletin announcement for the program's launch. You also should ask the priest if he would be willing to make an announcement from the pulpit at Mass informing men at the parish of the program.

Before your first group meeting, you should secure a meeting room or location that lends itself to protecting the privacy of the men. I recommend meeting once per month, for instance on the third Friday, from 6 to 7 am. (Typically few people are milling about at 6 am.)

For the first meeting, you can set the content of the meeting yourself, or you can use an existing program like my Brotherhood of Virtue program found in Lionheart Catholic. It contains videos that you and your group can watch each session, along with discussion questions. Often times, men have trouble opening up about this topic, because it is so shameful, so it is helpful to have something to discuss.

Each session should start with a prayer, then discuss whatever topic related to purity that you have come up with or have gotten from my video program. Next, you can have a time for accountability and sharing in the group for men who are comfortable doing that, then as a group, each man should commit to doing action items or resolutions from that day's lesson. Finally, I recommend praying the Rosary or Divine Mercy Chaplet to end the meeting.

In my experience, it is difficult to get men to come to the meetings. What I suggest is that you make up some simple business cards that contain the basic information about the group, what it is, when it meets, and contact information for you if they have any questions.

I printed out a stack of these business cards and handed them to our parish priest, asking him if he was willing to give them out to men in Confession. He agreed and has been handing out the cards ever since.

You do not have to have conquered these sins yourself to start such a group. Rather, it can be powerful when you yourself are going on this journey along with the other men in the group. Either way works, just know that you're not disqualified if you're struggling with these sins currently.

The Recipe of the Saints

The Bible
Eucharistic Adoration
Catechism of the Catholic Church
The Rosary
The Theology of the Body
Aquinas's Virtue Principles
Fasting
Novenas
Apologetics
Graciousness when under fire
Trust through trials
Uniting sufferings to Christ's
Happiness in the next life
Detachment from this world
Love of enemies
Selfless humility
Release control, do your best, and leave the results in
God's hands
Warm authenticity
Mental Prayer
Following God against opposition

CHAPTER 17

Following the Recipe

"Be watchful, stand firm in your faith, be courageous, be
strong. Let all that you do be done in love."
—1 Corinthians 16:13,14

A re you feeling overwhelmed yet?
I have now given you all of the ingredients that I have
discovered thus far in my life as a Catholic. These ingredients
can be mixed together to make the recipe that all the saints
followed.

I revealed these ingredients in the order in which I discovered them, but that is not the order that you should begin to
put them into practice.

Incorporating the Ingredients

Below I will tell you the order in which I think you should
incorporate the ingredients into your own life. Of course, every
person is different, and the Holy Spirit will direct you in what
you most need to be doing.

I first recommend that you begin practicing vocal prayer,
specifically the Rosary, every day. You will find it helpful to

choose a time and place to pray it each day: in the morning when you wake up, on your commute into work, or in the evening before bed, for instance. I always find it easier to pray the Rosary when I can pray it with someone else. If you have that option available, invite your friend or family member to pray it with you.

Next, I recommend you begin practicing mental prayer, which is the second level of prayer above vocal prayer, every day for five minutes.

I wished that I had discovered mental prayer early on in my life as a Catholic. Instead, it took over fifteen years for me to find it. There's an old saying that goes, "the best time to plant a tree was twenty years ago; the next best time is now."

That applies to mental prayer as well. There's no time like the present to start doing it. Mental prayer will form the crucial basis for all of the other practices you adopt and, truly, everything you do. Remember that every saint became a saint through mental prayer, so your journey to holiness will be no different in this regard.

Now you have the foundation of prayer in your life. If you're struggling with some habitual sin, through mental prayer and St. Thomas Aquinas's principles of virtues, you should work to conquer that sin.

Remember that St. Thomas demonstrated that growing strong in one virtue, will strengthen you in other virtues. For example, self-mastery in one area, say eating or exercising, will help you master yourself in areas where you are weak.

Let's take the example of the vice of lust. In addition to mental prayer and working to grow in opposing virtues, you can incorporate the Theology of the Body by reading about it, meditating on it, and putting it into practice in how you view the opposite sex. To further help you win this fight, I recommend adding fasting to your weekly regimen as well.

Now that you were working on these spiritual aspects of your life, we need to arm your intellect with the understanding of God's divine revelation.

That means that you should begin reading the Bible and the Catechism of the Catholic Church. I recommend following the "read-in-one-year" guides that I referenced in the chapters on these ingredients.

If you are dealing with specific attacks on your faith from others, whether atheist or Protestant or from some other source, you could begin to read specific books to help you defend your faith against those challenges. Either way, you want to practice graciousness under fire that the great saint apologists did.

To help you in your prayer life, I also recommend at this point that you sign up for a Holy Hour of Eucharistic Adoration. In addition to being a great place to practice mental prayer on the days you go to Adoration, you can also quietly pray your Rosary, and you can mix in the ingredient of novenas for specific intentions that you have.

In your life, on an ongoing basis, you are going to be facing various obstacles, trials, and sufferings. These are a part of life, and we can never wholly escape from them.

Because of this reality, be mindful to recognize when you are facing trials, and seek to practice the ingredients of trust, uniting your sufferings to those of Jesus, recalling that happiness will only be found in the next life and not in this one, practicing detachment from the world, loving your enemies, and seeing how you need to act in a humble and selfless way.

You will always need to practice those timeless virtues.

If you are a parent, work to communicate with your children and love them in an authentic and warm way. You are the image of God for them and their most compelling witness to the beauty, truth, and goodness of the Catholic Faith.

The last ingredient in our recipe is following God against opposition. You may not have to put this into practice too often. However it is good to keep in mind that you need to stay true to how our Lord is directing you in various ways in your life.

You want to be sure to do what is right and to persevere in it and not be dissuaded or deterred by even well-meaning people, even other Catholics, who begin to naysay or cause doubts for you.

This is the order in which I suggest you mix in the ingredients of the recipe of the saints. You may already have mastered some of these elements, or have been practicing them for a long time, in which case you can simply keep doing what you're doing with those and begin to incorporate the ingredients that you're not yet using.

It took me almost twenty years as a Catholic to start practicing all of these, so know that this may be the work of decades in your life as well.

The Sacraments and Service

I didn't include a chapter on receiving the sacraments, nor on specific ministries or apostolates that you could serve in, but that is not because they are unimportant. Quite the opposite.

Every saint made frequent use of the sacraments. They were initiated into the Catholic Church through Baptism, Confirmation, and the Eucharist. They went to Confession frequently. Some received the sacrament of Holy Orders and became priests and bishops. Others received the sacrament of Holy Matrimony.

It goes without saying that you should go to Mass every Sunday and Holy Day of Obligation. Not to do so (without a valid reason) puts your soul at peril and moves you *away* from becoming a saint!

Most saints went to daily Mass and received Jesus in the Eucharist as often as they could, and in doing so they were strengthened by God's grace. You should emulate them and do the same.

Of the sacraments, Holy Eucharist and Confession are the two that you should partake in as frequently as possible. This regimen is the spiritual foundation for your journey to becoming a saint. By ourselves we can do nothing, but with God's grace we can anything He wills.

Now let's talk about volunteering and doing service for the Kingdom. In following the recipe of the saints, you are being formed into the person God created you to be. He has definite plans for you, works that only you can do. Through mental prayer, following a spiritual director, and through the circumstances of your life, the Holy Spirit will show you how and where you should volunteer.

That may mean you join the St. Vincent de Paul Society chapter at your parish. It may mean you clean the altar linens, or arrange the books in the pews, or decorate the parish for liturgical seasons.

It may mean that you teach CCD at your parish or volunteer with the youth program. It might be instead that you join the Knights of Columbus and serve in that capacity, or that you become a Third Order Franciscan, or Lay Dominican, or Benedictine Oblate. The possibilities are almost endless in how you can follow our Lord in His Church. Within the unity of truth, great diversity of charism exists.

All the saints served our Lord in the Church and in the world in countless ways. You will, too. But in doing so, you can only give what you yourself have. If you have peace, you can give peace. If you have wisdom, you can give wisdom. If you have a solid foundation in prayer and understanding, you can help others form a strong foundation as well. Following the recipe of the saints will give you this foundation.

I can't wait to see where God leads you!

The Final Recipe of the Saints

1. The Rosary
2. Mental Prayer
3. Aquinas's Virtue Principles
4. The Theology of the Body
5. Fasting
6. The Bible
7. Catechism of the Catholic Church
8. Apologetics
9. Graciousness when under fire
10. Eucharistic Adoration
11. Novenas
12. Uniting sufferings to Christ's
13. Happiness in the next life
14. Detachment from this world
15. Love of enemies
16. Selfless humility
17. Trust through trials
18. Release control, do your best, and leave the results in God's hands
19. Warm authenticity
20. Following God against opposition

CHAPTER 18

The Lionheart Catholic

"Then one of the elders said to me, 'Weep not; lo, the Lion
of the tribe of Judah, the Root of David, has conquered, so
that he can open the scroll and its seven seals.'"
—Revelation 5:5

The Church is in crisis today.

And because of that, the world, too, is in crisis.

In responding to this crisis, you have three options: activism, passivism, or renewal. You could become an activist and start "doing" external things: protest the bishops, the pope, your diocese. Demand that "they" change and clean house (whatever that might mean).

Many people and groups have been practicing activism for the past seventy years. And they've won some small victories, but not nearly enough to slow, let alone stop, the avalanche of destruction that has led to the Church hemorrhaging members at an unprecedented pace.

Let's say you oust one bad bishop. Seven more, potentially even worse, are ready to take his place, and the same wonky principles that led to that bad bishop being appointed in the first place will ensure that another bad bishop likely gets the nod.

No, while protesting has its place, and each person can and should use his prudential judgment in deciding whether, for example, he gives any part of his tithe to the latest capital campaign from the diocese, protesting and activism and getting angry are not going to solve the problems.

What about passivism? What about shrugging one's shoulders and just plodding on ahead doing "business as usual?" Or, even worse, what about going along with the status quo, making excuses for the scandals and the state of the Church today?

That strategy does not work either. Doing the same thing that we've done for the past decades will clearly not result in a turnaround. What is that third option, the one I call renewal?

Quite simply, renewal is the option that I am putting into practice. It is the option that you have been discovering with me in this book, as one-by-one we have found the secret ingredients that all the saints lived out.

Renewal is taking action, though, make no mistake, it is not activism. Rather, renewal begins inside of yourself, and only from within then works its way out to affect the Church and then the world.

Renewal means becoming a saint. When we look at the past two thousand years of history, it has been the saints who have renewed the Church and transformed the world. This fact should not surprise us, since a saint is by definition someone who does God's will. In the Our Father, we pray "thy will be done on earth as it is in Heaven," so doing God's will is not just an empty hope, but rather is embedded in the very prayer that Jesus taught us to pray.

When we do God's will, great things happen. People's hearts and lives change. They are converted to the Catholic Faith; they leave their old ways of sin and begin to follow the truth.

Renewal is also different from Reformation. We don't need to re-form the Church that Christ already formed. The Protestant Reformation tried this, resulting in a schism from the Church that Christ established, which is never God's will.

Instead, like St. Francis of Assisi in the 1200s, when God told him to "repair my Church, which is falling into ruin," the saints renew the Church from within and spark movements, like the Franciscans and Dominicans, who eventually number in the hundreds, thousands, tens of thousands, and hundreds of thousands, as they fanned out around the world, bringing the Gospel of Jesus to the ends of the earth.

Renewal is what we need, and the secret recipe of the saints is what we need to follow in order to become saints and bring about that renewal. But we as Catholics are not Lone Rangers. We don't try to tackle the demons alone. Instead, we are strongest when we join together in fellowship, in encouragement, in sharing wisdom, and when we pray together, seeking to know how God is leading us.

One evening, I was reflecting on all of the secret ingredients that I had learned, and I prayed that God would direct me in how I could help to share these with other people. The first answer that I got was to write this book.

But the next answer was to go beyond a book and form a group of champions for Christ, lion-hearted men and women from every country and continent, all who share the same goal: to become saints, renew the Church, and transform the world.

Lionheart Catholic was born. A Lionheart is someone who is courageous, a noble champion or hero, and that is what I envisioned us being for Christ.

Do you want to become a saint?

Do you want to renew the Church?

Do you want to be a champion for Christ?

Then you want to be a Lionheart Catholic.

We are nothing on our own, but with Christ's grace, the guidance of the Church, and the encouragement of one another, we can accomplish the high calling that God gives us. Instead of trying to figure out everything on your own, by joining together, we will accelerate our growth in holiness, and our efforts to renew the Church from within.

I wish that I had had someone to guide me in such a way, or even to share my journey with, but it simply didn't exist as I was going through these experiences. Now, it does exist. If the secret ingredients of the saints resonate with you, if you want to put them into practice in your life and learn from others who are on the same journey, then consider becoming one of Christ's Lionhearts.

I'll see you on the inside.

God bless,
Devin

P.S. You can learn more here: https://lionheartcatholic.com